Ranking Number One

50 Essential SEO Tips to Boost Your Search Engine Results

by James Beswick

Published by One Uproar, a DBA of 415 Systems, Inc.

PRINTING HISTORY:

JUNE 2010:   FIRST EDITION

ISBN: 978-1-452849904

Printed in the United States

About the Author

James Beswick has a B.Sc. in Management and Computer Science from Royal Holloway College, University of London. James is also Google Analytics IQ Certified.

He has worked for a variety of Fortune 500 companies and consults in online marketing, search engine optimization and website design. James has a keen interest in technology and marketing, and aims to help organizations to maximize their revenue opportunities online. James also provides webinars and seminars to small and medium-sized businesses to help them get the most out of SEO and online marketing.

Also by this author: *"Getting Productive With Google Apps"*, published in January 2009.

Acknowledgments

Thanks to everyone in the SEO community for continuously providing their insight and feedback into this ever-changing industry, and for my clients for providing the opportunity to put SEO practices to work and experiment with the many ideas and theories circulating out there.

Thanks to my wife, Wendy, for all her support and for proof-reading this manuscript.

Contact the author

Please email james@ranking-number1.com with your questions, comments and errata.

Visit **http://www.ranking-number1.com** for additional content, updates and resources.

CONTENTS

BEFORE YOU START

SITE DESIGN

ON-PAGE FACTORS

OFF-PAGE FACTORS

MORE SEO TECHNIQUES

Introduction

The speed of development of the web is staggering, isn't it? 15 years ago, very few people had email. 10 years ago, most people didn't have wireless. A couple of years ago, hardly any of my family or friends were on Facebook and Twitter was a fringe community. How times change. What we're seeing is a full-on transformation in the way that we all communicate and search for things that's evolving exponentially. If you're in business and you have a website you cannot afford to ignore these changes embraced by your market.

If you've ever searched for anything on the web, you know its power. As a user, you likely have good skills in terms of finding what you want, from books and DVDs to delivery pizza and gardening advice. But as a business or website manager, your thinking may be behind the curve. Visitors don't want stale 1995-era static sites but rich, useful content that solves their immediate needs. And this is where SEO comes in, since it can connect the search engines that visitors use with the site you have created.

SEO stands for **Search Engine Optimization**. Although it's treated like some sort of voodoo in some circles, it's actually the practice of giving the search engines the best possible interpretation of your site and therefore giving your site the best possible chance of ranking well. This book provides 50 SEO tips that can be implemented on almost any site to provide an advantage in search engine ranking, but many of which are still not practiced by even the largest and most successful websites.

There are many search engines out there - Google, Yahoo! and Bing being the largest, but there are hundreds of others. Each has it own particular way of working, but the majority of these tips will be applicable to all. Since Google represents the lion's share of search, and the big three service the vast majority of search requests, focusing on Google, then Yahoo! and then Bing serves as a good strategy for most sites.

Is SEO free?

Due to the rising cost of paid search campaigns, there's been a renewed focus on *organic results*, which are the listings provided by search engines for free. Instead of paying for your ad to appear on the ubiquitous sidebars and paying per click, organic results can provide the equivalent of a free billboard for your organization or business. And who doesn't want free advertising in business?

Of course, there is no such thing as a free lunch. While you don't pay for the organic listings, it takes more time, effort and skill to appear in these results than simply developing search advertisements. In some respects, what you save in avoiding PPC advertising you pay for in the time and effort required to make your site rank well. And SEO is no longer all about just your site - it's about how others link to you, how you maintain your online reputation through social media, and how you interact with your customers, industry and community. There are many more moving parts in SEO that have to be managed to retain a page one ranking.

No Tricks, No Voodoo

Before we get started, there are a few things that are worth mentioning in the world of SEO. Contrary to the advice of some of the less ethical operators on the web, there are no tricks, shortcuts or back doors that will work for any period of time to make your site rank well. While ranking on the first page of Google is the Holy Grail for anyone with a website, it takes patience, hard work and common sense to have the honor of the first page - and to maintain it.

Ranking on the first page of a search engine essentially means your page is one of the ten best available on the entire web, taking into account the search phrase used and - more commonly - the geographic source of the search request. To be considered one of the ten most relevant sources for a query is no small task considering the billions of pages on the web, and since it's a dynamic environment, your position can change at any moment in time. Thinking about your content, you have to prove to the engines *continuously* that your pages are worthy of a top listing.

Most of the bad advice the SEO community has heard over the years hasn't stood the test of time. Search engines used to be easily misled due to technical limitations so websites peddling multi-level marketing, porn and scams could invade the search results for innocuous search terms. Today, that couldn't be further from the truth: Google in particular updates its indexing algorithm (GoogleBot) 'very often'. Nobody outside Google knows for sure but some speculate that it gets changed daily, weekly or multiple times a month. Regardless of the frequency, this means it generally gets better all the time, so forget the tricks!

Little Insider Knowledge, More Experimentation

The voodoo aspect of SEO stems from one simple problem: nobody knows the proprietary methods used by search engines to index websites. SEO techniques evolve from a combination of backwards engineering and listening to the few people working for search engines who throw out the occasional pieces of advice. As a result, search engine optimizers don't agree on everything, since practices stem from a mixture of science, computer knowledge, marketing and results from experience. Due to the fact that much of SEO is a grey area, I've focused on generally agreed principals and flagged contentious issues throughout this book where appropriate.

We're all listening for insider advice constantly. People such as Matt Cutts, who has become one of the most famous 'Matts' on the entire web, are watched like hawks by the SEO community. Matt is a particular good example, since his advice is always good to follow and not intended to mislead anyone wanting higher rankings. It's a myth that search engines dislike SEO - they actually encourage it, purely because it's a win-win for everyone involved. Since this isn't a static environment, if you're serious about SEO and keeping your website ranking well, it's important to stay current with what people like Matt are saying. I've listed sources later in this book that continue to provide up-to-date information that will help you stay on top of how search engines are thinking.

In one respect, there isn't much magic to search engines from the perspective as a user. If you've Googled, Yahoo'd or Bing'd much, you'll quickly see there's intense competition to give their users the best possible results based upon search phrases. Google talks about timeliness and relevance being their major drivers in their results, and it shows when you use their service - if the results were not on target, visitors would quickly start going elsewhere for information. This means we know from the start that timeliness and relevance are the goals we should strive for above all else to achieve a top ranking, and the rest will come.

Of course, there is some magic since search engine spiders - the programs that ultimately find, index and rank your site - are just software, but *very* sophisticated software processing billions of frequently changing web pages. They've evolved to understand semantics so they know that "dog" and "doggy" are the same thing and "dog" and "poodle" are closely related. They also realize how topics and subjects connect with each other, so that sites about "hot dogs" are discussing food rather than poodles needing air conditioning. In building an SEO strategy, you have to consider how your site fits into the web of existing content, and how to convince the spiders that your site is the most relevant for user queries.

Rapid Tips Delivered Quickly

While there are few guarantees in SEO, I do guarantee you this: implementing the tips in a determined and constructive way will absolutely improve your search rankings. You have an opportunity to propel your site into the page one rankings of SERPs (search engine results pages) and compete with larger players in a way that wouldn't be possible in any other medium without a huge budget.

In this book, I aim to give you the fast track to SEO success in terms of learning how to use a range of tried-and-tested techniques. There is no fast track in terms of suddenly becoming number one, but as with most things in life persistence and consistency will get you there in the end. I decided to break the content into 50 tips so you can read any particular one at random and get results, but you're also more than welcome to read cover to cover.

Additionally, I've added screenshots wherever it makes the content faster to understand, and broken most major issues into bullet points to help you get the information you need more quickly. There are also resources featuring blog posts and additional reading - since these external links can change without notice, they are kept up to date on the book's website (**http://ranking-number1.com**). This style should help to convey the most important elements as quickly as possible.

Before we get into the detail, I'd suggest taking the following general approach in your SEO effort:

- **Respect the search engines**: they use sophisticated algorithms written by smart people to provide billions of users with helpful results every second of every day. Don't try to game them.

- **Be search-engine friendly**: so many sites are not that you'll quickly gain a competitive advantage by working constructively with the engines.

- **Build a great site**: websites are not marketing brochures. Make great content, do it often, and both visitors and search engines will hold your site in high regard.

- **Focus on content**: the same reason why you visit a site repeatedly is the same reason your visitors will become loyal to your site - content is truly King.

Finally, writing a book is no small task and I'm always interested in hearing your success stories - and the stories that didn't work out so well. If you have comments, questions or need further advice, drop me an email. In the meantime, let's start at the beginning and focus on getting your site to the top!

James Beswick
james@ranking-number1.com

BEFORE YOU START

Most tips throughout this book can be applied to a site 'in progress', but if you're planning to either redesign your entire online presence or do something dramatic, this section provides advice at the broader level.

Here we cover:

- Setting goals and taking stock of your existing website: discover what you're trying to achieve and learn where what you currently have falls short.
- The pros and cons of site design: what you should focus on and what you should avoid.
- Site hosting: the ideal attributes of a good web host, and why quality hosting services affect your SEO.
- The importance of keywords: knowing what your competitors are targeting as well as making conscious and data-driven decisions about your own keywords.
- Pitfalls: some so-called 'blackhat' SEO tips that you should avoid.

In a perfect world, SEO should be built-in to a website from the ground-up. It's harder to retrofit SEO techniques into an existing site, but if you are starting from scratch with SEO in mind then you're in a great position to rank well.

01 **Set your SEO goals**

Before undertaking any major overhaul of your site, be sure to set specific goals.

Most people and organizations end up interested in SEO because they've built a website and the masses have not arrived. A web page without SEO is like the proverbial tree falling in the forest when nobody hears it. Developing SEO goals into your site design from the very beginning will help avoid the panic of creating a beautiful looking site that gets ignored by search engines and traffic.

How do you measure the popularity of a website? Unlike the offline world, online resources - such as web pages, white papers or ads - are highly trackable, so it's easy to see when a $50,000 website is only receiving a handful of visitors per day. But while traffic, hits, clicks and customers are talked about in the same breath, they are all very different metrics, and it's possible to optimize for each one separately.

What are your SEO goals? Here are some ideas:

- To increase the number of **unique visitors** to your site.
- To increase the number of **page views**.
- To decrease the **bounce rate** (the number of visitors who view a single page and then exit the site completely).
- To increase the number of **pages viewed per visit**.
- To increase visits or views to a particular **landing page**.
- To **convert** more visitors to customers.
- To **increase sales** on your site.

In considering your goals, you have to realistically assess your resources in terms of time and expenditure and decide which are attainable. For example, a paid search campaign is the fastest way to drive traffic to a particular landing page, but if the landing page is poor at converting clicks to customers, then paying $5 per click would likely not be the best strategy.

Maybe the number of visitors to your site is not the problem, but each visitor is only staying for a short period before leaving (all of these statistics can be collected using applications such as Google Analytics - see tip 42). The strategy could be to encourage these visitors to stay longer by potentially changing the navigation system or page content, or providing incentives to hang around.

Most sites have their own set of distinct SEO goals - without goals in mind, you can optimize your site but will find it hard to measure its success against anything. While it's great to appear on page one of Google's search results for your chosen keywords, if this ranking doesn't translate to greater traffic or sales then it's something of a Pyrrhic victory.

A client ranked number one for her company name but was nowhere to be seen for the description of her product "frozen sushi". The problem with choosing your company name as primary keywords is that unless you're a well-known brand, visitors are more likely to search for your product or service than the name "Oregon's Premium Sushi Co".

Making your goals SMART

You should discuss with your sales, marketing and executive teams what your SEO and broader website goals are, and perhaps include an SEO consultancy for guidance (see tip 48 on how to get external help). However you choose those targets, I recommend taking the SMART approach used in project management, which will help ensure relevance and measurability. Make your goals:

- **Specific**: don't be too broad in a target, and keep it simple (e.g. increase new accounts).

- **Measurable**: select a target that can be measured now and at the end of the project (e.g. increase new accounts by 25%).

- **Attainable**: ensure the goal is achievable - trying to become the next Facebook is probably not attainable for most organizations.

- **Relevant**: ensure the goal is realistic and specific to what SEO can achieve. Improving logistics and customer satisfaction may not be directly related to your website.

- **Time-bound**: all goals should have a deadline (e.g. increase sales by 25% in the next 6 months).

It may take several iterations to find the metrics that make sense for your site, and these will help you discover the return on investment for your online strategy. The offline media world has traditionally incorporated ROI, but found the results harder to prove. Online media has rapidly adopted similar measures to determine profitability but has the advantage that the tracking tools and real-time capability to change content enable endless experimentation to develop the best strategy.

For some additional ideas, see http://www.seoboy.com/unsexy-seo/setting-seo-goals.

02 **Evaluate your existing web site**

Once your goals are established, analyze where your existing online presence falls short.

Web presence encompasses everything you are online: your website, social media accounts, integration with product databases (such as Google Base), payment platforms and anything else that can be reached in a browser. After setting your SEO goals, the next step is to the take stock of your web presence and determine what works, what's broken and what can be improved.

Building a new website is not the answer to SEO unless you have specifically determined that the existing site is beyond repair. You can't effectively decide on a course of action unless you carry out a thorough inventory of everything you already have. In working this out, collect statistics where possible, gather feedback from customers and site visitors, and interview vendors and coworkers to discover where your online strengths and weaknesses lie.

In this phase, you may discover that:

- The site only works in a **couple of browsers** that many of your visitors don't use.
- The **site's navigation** is confusing or complicated.
- You have resources missing or **broken links**.
- Your **content is irrelevant**, unnecessary or fails to engage the audience.
- The **site is unattractive** and outdated.
- You offer **limited payment options** that your customers don't want (eg. PayPal only and no credit cards), or your payment area doesn't look secure and users don't trust the site.
- You are receiving **substantial negative feedback** about your products or services within the social media networks, and not addressing these criticisms effectively.
- The site doesn't appear on search engines, and **nobody mentions your site** anywhere else.
- Your content is "**spammy**" or too sales-oriented.

Once you have completed the assessment, you should be able to draw up a list of problem areas. Whether you decide to revamp your web presence from scratch or make incremental improvements, it's critical that you address these problems in the project. There's not much point in investing time and effort into renovating your online identity only to find your new site has the same problems as before but with a different look.

I worked for a company that wanted a complete site refresh since 0% of site visitors were converting into sales, and shopping carts were being abandoned. In evaluating their site, I discovered the shopping cart's "Checkout" button was a broken link, making it impossible to buy anything online.

Evaluating your web presence

Your industry or profession will determine the basic expectations of your customer base for your online presence: dentists and book stores are clearly not expected to offer the same features and services online.

Consequently, it pays to thoroughly assess your competitors' online capabilities, and decide which elements are worth implementing (such as booking or paying online, tracking shipments, sharing with other customers through forums, etc.) Spending time to judge their strengths will help in deciding where your online capabilities are currently deficient - or superior.

The second step is to move beyond what your competitors are currently doing online. This is a more difficult phase, but can yield significant results. The aim here is to see what works in other industries (and is technically possible) and can be translated to your industry to give your business a competitive advantage. This requires some lateral thinking, but what's to say the features that make larger websites more successful couldn't meet the needs of your customers?

- **Dell Outlet's** Twitter account (**http://twitter.com/dellOutlet**) offers deals on refurbished hardware and excess inventory unavailable on their main site (and has over 1.5 million followers). Would your customers be interested in one-of-a-kind instant Twitter deals?

- **My Starbucks Idea** (**http://mystarbucksidea.force.com/ideaHome**) took ideas from customers, measured the popular ones through crowd-sourcing and showed their progress in development. Do you have customers that would like to contribute ideas to your product for free? Can you engage them?

- **The Luxor Las Vegas** uses Twitter to aggregate customer recommendations and push them out to visitors in real-time. Are you in an industry where real-time feedback can create a better experience for your customers?

For ideas and inspiration, see Mashable's 40 Best Twitter Brands: http://mashable.com/2009/01/21/best-twitter-brands.

Redesigning to boost business

oid specious reasons for redesigning your website,
ch as changing layouts and design. The main reason
is to generate more leads, customers and sales.

Let's repeat this point again, since it's the number one waste of website design money in the marketplace. Websites get branded and rebranded, built and rebuilt for the best of intentions, rarely of which consider the main reason for the website's existence in the first place. As with any other type of marketing, website design should have an expected *return on investment* (which is measurable from your goals in tip 1).

Unless you're Amazon.com or Overstock.com, and need to trial legitimate testing scenarios (and those sites really understand user testing), you should only be working on website redesign for the express purpose of increasing leads and customer conversions. Of course, you may also want to improve the existing customers' experience or create communities to drive online product awareness, but these goals ultimately create leads, sales and more customers.

Usually, the number one goal is to attract more visitors, which in turn generates leads, which - hopefully - become customers (or at the very least followers on Twitter, Facebook or email newsletter subscribers). The only reason to change the design, layout or appearance of the site is if you can demonstrably prove that it will boost visitor numbers (to lift leads and customer conversions). Most organizations that become interested in SEO are attempting some form of site renovation. This is perfectly healthy, and it's great many companies are open to changing fundamental parts of their online presence, but improving SEO must be linked to building business from the outset.

How do you know which elements of a site redesign will attract more visitors? This largely comes from examining existing keywords, finding new keywords (and phrases) you're not targeting, and looking at user behavior. Are your visitors staying for a long time on your site or leaving immediately? How many pages do they view? Do they come back? Before even beginning the journey of optimizing for search engines, it starts with understanding three things:

- Who are your existing and potential customers?
- What information are they searching for?
- Is your site meeting their needs?

Focus on content not layout

95% of most web design budgets are invested in converting a paper brochure into a website. Instead, 95% should go into the content that will *wow* your visitors.

Much like a failing newspaper that sees a new page layout as its salvation, most companies renovate with a focus on design rather than content. As web users, we're all adept at finding the content that matches our search - we know that the only value of a site is in answering our questions. Yet as web designers, technologists and marketing departments, we honestly believe that our site will be different - the amazing design will compensate for the thin content and magnetize users to the site. This is dead wrong - for a successful website renovation, you must focus on content rather than design.

For this reason, I'd recommend starting with a template. There are tens of thousands of templates on the web, and one of these will look more professional than whatever you pay somebody to design. This doesn't mean you can't start with an existing design and make custom modifications, but starting from scratch is usually a terrible idea. Here's why:

- **Many great templates** are already SEO optimized, tested across multiple browsers, have liquid layouts (they work for variable screen widths - see tip 26), are sitemap-friendly and basically popular. Can you produce a layout of this quality on your budget?

- Using a template prevents the urge to **convert print materials into websites** - these are two different media and this mistake is tantamount to taking a flyer and making it a TV commercial.

- Users are getting very familiar with the general way that **website navigation works** (hierarchical menus, navigation at the top, etc.) Why reinvent the wheel and produce a site that confuses your users by not meeting their expectations?

- Many templates get the **technical aspects** of web page design right such as HTML and CSS validation. It's surprising how many web designers don't.

Layout and redesign should represent a tiny amount of any website renovation work, while your biggest concern must be content. Without compelling content, you cannot and will not rank on the first page for your chosen search terms, nor will your traffic convert into sales. Yet great content almost puts your SEO on autopilot, quality links will start to appear and visitors will be flocking to your site. Content is King - the downside is that creating compelling content requires time, creativity, consistency and an ability to see your product or service from a customer's perspective.

For 50 Content Ideas that Create Buzz, see http://www.conversationagent. com/2009/04/50-content-ideas-the-create-buzz.html.

04 **Address site redesign problems**

Change is often good but in website redesign it more often results in lower search engine rankings, confused visitors and broken links.

There are many ways in which changing your website could have negative consequences on SEO - and it can frequently cause a drop in keyword rankings and a loss of inbound links. This is especially true if an existing site has been in place for a long time because your site already contains collateral that is indexed and linked to from third parties (inbound links) and these pages are frequently lost in redesigns. Many web design companies don't put adequate effort into preserving existing links and pages that are performing well in search.

You need to carefully evaluate your existing site to discover which pages, resources and assets are being valued by users and search engines, and make sure these don't disappear without warning. This doesn't mean the design cannot change, but it does mean some housekeeping such as providing redirects - the technical equivalent of a change of address form at the post office. This means that when a user (or search engine) goes to **http://mysite.com/great_ideas.html** and it has subsequently become **http://mysite.com/ideas/great.asp**, they can still find what they are looking for.

Don't move the existing assets without warning - this causes the dreaded "404 error", which is an Internet euphemism for "not here". Since SEO is all about content, and content attracts search engine spiders - which in turn bring visitors - removing valuable content without warning is one of the most damaging things you can do.

Make sure your designers guarantee that every resource will be redirected effectively and no resource will be unreachable due to address changes or basic removal. Always perform an inventory of web pages that are currently indexed and have inbound links, and ensure that 301 redirects are in place to politely inform spiders and other sites of the changes. And once the new site is completed, test to ensure the redirects are actually there.

> I worked with one site whose bounce rate increased to nearly 90% following a site overhaul. Traffic was cut in half and search engine rankings deteriorated for months afterwards. They had changed their domain name and site navigation and failed to implement any redirects.

Changing Navigation

Regular visitors come to learn the navigation on your site, even if the existing navigation isn't great. Moving web pages around has a tendency to confuse your loyal visitor base, and since the average time spent on a web page is merely seconds (and getting shorter), visitors will often give up rather than try to find what used to be there.

As visitors sometimes bookmark their favorite sites, such as your login page or product catalog, always make sure that old URLs resolve correctly to their new location (e.g. **http://login.mysite.com** still works after moving to **http://mysite.com/login**).

Changing Domain Names

Moving a new domain name is dangerous, and should really only happen if you have no investment in an old domain name, or you are moving from shared hosting (e.g. **http://mycompany.wordpress.com**) to your own domain - and only then if it's managed very carefully. Switching from **http://mycompany.com** to **http://mykeywords.com** is fraught with difficulties and you should balance any potential upside with the likely massive downside.

Why is this such a problem? Imagine a company with 5 years of online reputation, inbound links, search engine indexing, and so forth. When you switch domain names, you are effectively shutting down this history and starting from zero, resulting in:

- **Search rankings** being reset, and potentially leaving SERPs altogether.
- **Link popularity** is not transferable, so you start over with the new domain.
- **A decline in traffic** - possibly a 50-90% drop in the search engines if the old links are now dead and the engines have not indexed the new site.
- **Losing the authority** associated with older domains by replacing it with a newly registered name (a domain first registered 5 years ago has a greater weighting than a younger domain - see tip 6).

You *must* implement 301 redirects from the old domain to the new domain or will lose absolutely all of your online reputation associated with your site. Domain migration is so difficult to manage from an SEO standpoint that for most businesses it's not worth doing at all.

For ideas on minimize traffic loss after a domain name change, see http://www.highrankings.com/faq-domain-change.

05 **Choosing a domain name**

Domain names are critical and including keywords in your name is often more valuable than the name itself.

Choosing your domain name, rather like choosing your business name or book title, is one of the most important parts of going online. From a visitor standpoint, shorter names are better, so companies such as CNN and Coke undoubtedly receive more direct traffic as a result, with users finding it easy to remember **http://cnn.com** or **http://coke.com**. But unless you're a recognizable brand, chances are that a short name doesn't cause much direct traffic, so we're back to relying on search engines to bring page views.

Most businesses register their names directly because it *is* their trading name - it's more obvious to be johndoughs.com than bestlocalpizza.com from the point of view of real people seeing the site. But from an SEO perspective, bestlocalpizza.com is the better domain to have if the targeted search keywords are 'best local pizza'.

The dilemma is that so many domain names are registered by spammers and companies intending to sell the names to third parties that your keyword-rich domain may not be available, or - if you wanted to buy at a third party - could cost anything from $10 to millions of dollars. Whether this investment is worthwhile depends upon your business, but many websites have had considerable success from just using their keyword phrase as the domain name (such as cheapflights.com).

Where a domain name contains multiple keywords, there are two schools of thought on whether the name should appear as one long word or be separated with dashes to help search engines identify the keywords (e.g. bestlocalpizza.com vs best-local-pizza.com). While it may be true that there is a slight SEO advantage with dashes, it's actually more confusing to human visitors to remember. If possible, it might be worth registering both versions, using the non-hyphenated version for your site, and having the hyphenated version redirected. From Google Analytics, you will be able to detect which is most popular over time.

If you haven't named your business yet, consider embedding keywords and the location into your real business title, such as ABC's Web Hosting (New York), and make sure you use keyword phrases where the domain names are readily available. While you probably wouldn't use the location in the domain name because it makes the name too long, it may help your ranking on services such as Google Maps where location is a major SEO factor.

Essential tips for finding a good domain name

Consider the following when purchasing domain names:

- Always purchase from a **reputable big-name registrar** (such as Name.com, GoDaddy, etc.) When you've invested time and money in a domain, you need to trust the registrar to maintain registration in a responsible way.

- Many offer an option called '**Private WHOIS**', either for free or a nominal charge. This hides the details of the owner, which prevents spam from companies harvesting the WHOIS database.

- While including keywords is good, **limit the length** of your chosen domain (and the number of hyphens), or search engines may consider the site spam. For instance, http://best-cheapest-shoes-discount-footwear.com is obviously designed to trick search engines, and they will penalize such sites. 10-12 characters should be considered a maximum length.

- **Be memorable**: as always, make it easy on your target audience - names such as petesperfect-purplepizza.com are hard to remember.

- **Creating completely new words** is great for branding but will take more effort to build an online presence. If you're inventive, you can find short domains this way. Although it will require more work initially to get brand recognition and become memorable, in the longer term it may form the foundation of a very solid brand - such as hulu.com or bibo.com.

- **Don't abuse copyright** or trademarks owned by others: you will eventually lose the domain and reset your SEO strategy to zero.

At domain registrars such as **http://name.com**, you can search for available domains based upon keywords and phrases. In addition to the .com extensions most users are familiar with, you may want to buy other extensions based upon your country of operation or other intended usage. For example, if you ever plan to operate in the UK, you should invest in the co.uk extension. Some of the more esoteric externsions, such as .me and .info are usually not worth buying.

Most registrars will allow you to search based upon keywords, so if your first choice isn't available, there are usually others that will work. You can buy as many domain names as you want, provided you pay the annual registration fee to maintain ownership, but the goal for most sites should be to buy one great name that is memorable, contains relevant keywords where possible, and can be used to build and market their brand.

See http://www.seomoz.org/blog/how-to-choose-the-right-domain-name for 12 Rules on Choosing the Right DomainName.

06 **Domain age and expiration**

Just like any real business, age matters for a domain name - older sites have more credibility. But unlike real businesses, there's also a stated expiration.

Search engines like to see that your domain name has history, since spammers frequently register and then quickly release domains. The theory goes that the older the domain, the more credible the site.

There are some in the SEO community who play down its importance, but one of Google's patents refers to domain age as a valid signal to determine site relevance. Consequently, others conclude it plays a significant part in the ranking algorithm. The problem is that domains can be registered for years but contain no site content (parked domains), so if age is used by search engines there are certainly other factors to consider its relevance rather than just the date alone.

Admittedly, you don't have much control over the age. With a brand new domain name, there's not much you can do about the creation date since it's set at the moment of registration. But you don't always have to purchase new since there is a secondary market in existing domains, which enables the new owners to take advantage of aged domains. You can find these through most major domain registrars, such as Name.com and they also trade in auctions like eBay.com.

Whereas a brand new domain usually costs between $7-12 a year, the price of existing domains can vary widely. The only caveat to purchasing an existing domain is to carry out due diligence to ensure it hasn't been part of a 'bad neighborhood' - inheriting sites with a history of spam or phishing will definitely not help SEO.

To find out when a domain was first created, go to **http://whois.net** and enter the name in the search field:

- **Created Date** shows the birthday of the domain and tells search engines how long the site has been in existence.
- **Expiration Date** indicates when the registration will lapse and the name will be deleted.

If you're already committed to a 'young' domain name, even though you can't change its age, you can extend its expiration. By default, most registrars bill their customers for the next 1 or 2 years, but you can optionally pay up to 10 years in advance (and at $7-12 a year, this is a reasonable investment).

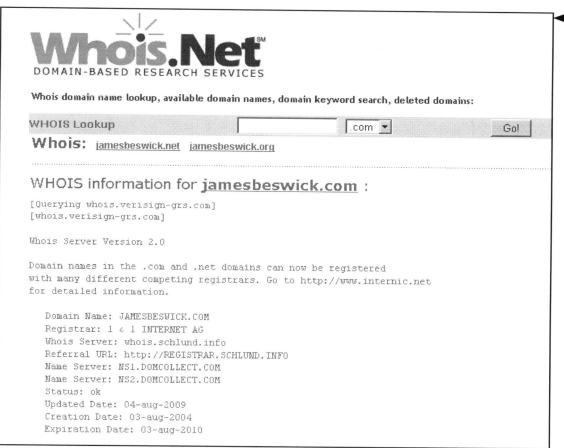

http://whois.net shows registration information about the domain name, including the creation and expiration dates.

Nobody knows for sure the significance of domain age and expiration in search engine rankings, but my opinion is that it doesn't hurt to register the next 5-10 years if you have an established business that plans to operate for the foreseeable future. A longer domain expiration demonstrates a commitment to search engines that the site will be around for a while, so even if there's only a small SEO benefit, it's probably worth the investment.

For more about domain age and expiration, see:
- http://www.bookmarkbliss.com/domain-names/does-domain-expiry-date-really-matter/
- http://www.searchenginejournal.com/domain-age-how-important-is-it-for-seo/7296/

07 Use reliable hosting services

Hosting affects the speed, uptime and reliability of your site so choose a hosting service that represents your own site's level of quality.

A quick Google search on 'hosting services' yields thousands of results, with prices starting at 'free' or a few dollars per month, and many promising "unlimited bandwidth and storage". As with so many things, you get what you pay for.

A $5/month hosting service may be fine if you are using the space for testing, or only have a small site with little traffic. These services work by sharing a server with hundreds (sometimes thousands) of customers, so the performance of the server and your site is subject to what other people's sites are doing on the same computer. If your site is for a business, the chances are that you will need a more robust host.

There are several broad types of host:

- **Shared hosting**: as described above, this is usually the cheapest solution but the least reliable. You are sharing a server with an unknown number of other sites.

- **Dedicated hosting**: the server is reserved for your use only - as you might expect, this is significantly more expensive.

- **Cloud-based (clustered) hosting**: a newer entrant in the market, this is a hybrid option that scales the number of servers depending on your bandwidth and CPU usage.

If you search for reviews of hosting companies, you will quickly get a feel of the relative service levels of different vendors. In hosting, cheap and big often do not usually equate to responsive and stable so choose wisely. Make sure the company hosts sites similar to your's, and find out what those customers think of their hosting. This is a good way to discover any hidden problems, such as extreme latency, server unavailability or billing issues.

The reason why hosting matters from an SEO standpoint is that if your site is unavailable when search engines visit, this hurts your ranking. But more importantly, visitors don't return to sites that are unavailable, so all your effort to attract new traffic will be wasted if your platform is unreliable.

When talking to web design professionals, one of the most common questions I get asked is "What host do you use?" Everyone wants the perfect host.

Top features you need in a web host

Finding reliable web hosting companies can take time, so here are some of the main features you should focus on to weed out the good from the bad:

- **24-hour support**: the web is a 24/7 marketplace and websites can have issues at any time of the day. When a server crashes at 3am, it's essential to have a phone number that will be answered immediately by someone with deep technical knowledge. It pays to place a few test calls to companies before moving your site to their servers.

- **Reasonable pricing**: the web is awash with $5/month hosts that any company with a serious approach to online marketing should avoid. These hosts operate by loading hundreds – sometimes thousands – of clients onto a single machine, and your site's performance will be at the mercy of those other sites. In quality hosting, low pricing should not be a priority.

- **Automatic backups**: there are many things that can go wrong on websites, so it's essential to take daily backups. Good hosting companies offer daily or even hourly back up services.

- **Clear uptime guarantees**: most services offer 99.9% uptime, which sounds great but in reality means your site will be unavailable for up to 87 hours a year. In some cases this may be acceptable but for a busy e-commerce site, 99.99% would be the minimum target.

- **Unlimited email**: many hosts place restrictions on the number of emails each account can send. While a restriction of 10,000 per day may be reasonable, there are services that limit the site to 50 per day and delete the rest. Establish what the limits are before opening an account.

- **SSL capabilities**: you may not need any secure pages initially but it's reasonably likely that at some point you will. SSL is more complicated to set up than you might think, so selecting a company that is comfortable with SSL certificates will make the process smoother.

- **Cpanel administration**: this is a widely established administration tool for Linux servers that handles everything from email routing to application installation. Cpanel is a fairly simple visual interface, a major time saver and outperforms competing administration tools.

- **Unlimited options**: make sure your host allows unlimited databases, email accounts, subdomains and FTP accounts. Unlimited bandwidth and disk storage are useful, but there's always a limitation in the fine print.

- **Being the actual web host**: there is a large industry in reselling web services and it can be difficult to determine if you are working with the host itself or a reseller. The major problem with resellers is that support issues can take longer to resolve and sometimes the reselling company is not familiar with the technology.

29

08 **Analyze competitor keywords**

SEO is about keyword competition: find out what your competitors are targeting before selecting your own.

Keywords are everything in search - when you open Google and search for something, those few words you type are the major determinant in the listings that follow. While it's true that there are many other factors, your choice in keywords (and keyword phrases) will critically affect the traffic you receive.

You will need to decide on your keyword terms, but you should check what keywords your competitors are using before finalizing your own list. Attempting to market your website without knowing the competitive landscape is a "fingers crossed" approach that rarely works.

Why do competitors' keywords matter?

- They may have more experience in online marketing, and have already found some of the problems you haven't encountered yet.

- They may have less experience and are making mistakes, such as missing obvious keyword phrases, that you can capitalize on to funnel traffic to your site.

- You can discover which keywords they tried to rank for, compared with which phrases they ended up ranking for, which may be different. A car dealer website attempting to rank for certain brands may end up ranking for "car dealers", "European car models" or some other phrase.

Bear in mind that competitor research is an intelligence-gathering exercise - the goal is to find niches and opportunities, not to merely copy keyword lists. When you look at several competitors, it's easier to build a list of which keywords they are commonly targeting, and gauge where the heaviest competition is for those keywords. Going head-to-head with the same keyword phrases is an uphill battle: ideally you seek niche phrases for your business that others are not competing for.

How do you do this? It's possible to do it manually through a combination of:

- Studying their HTML, site map and internal links on their site: which phrases are they obviously targeting and what anchor text in their internal links is being reinforced?

- Examining their inbound links and checking the anchor text phrases commonly used.

- If they have a paid search campaigns, examining which keyword phrases trigger their ads (since many sites simply replicate the same keyword phrases in their paid marketing).

This can be lengthy and painstaking, so it's fortunate there are some automated tools that not only speed up the process but provide additional metrics too. KeywordSpy, SpyFu and SEO Digger are all excellent for this purpose. SEO Digger provides a truncated free report, as shown below.

SEO Digger for quick competitive analysis

Go to **http://seodigger.com** and enter the competitor site you want to analyze:

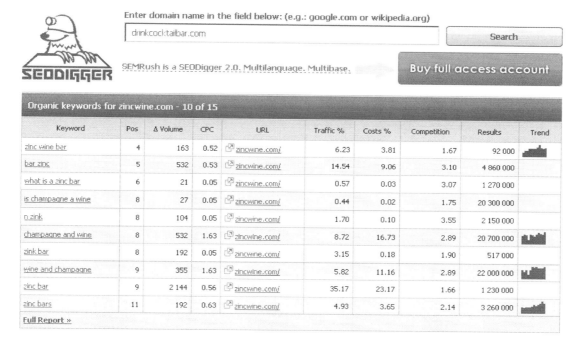

In addition to showing their targeted keywords, SEO Digger returns several other useful metrics, showing Google search volume for the terms, effectiveness and competitiveness:

- **Position**: for each phrase, the site's placement in Google's results.
- **Volume**: the number of times the phrase was searched for by Google users in the last month.
- **Traffic**: how much each phrase contributed to drawing visitors from Google.
- **Competition**: the higher the number, the more competition for the search term.
- **Results**: the number of pages that Google indexes for the given query.

The best keywords to target have both high search volume *and* low competition.

09 Selecting your keywords

Before building anything, it's essential to select your keyword list. Without strong, effective keywords and phrases, traffic won't find you.

Search engines are keyword driven. When you search with Google, Yahoo! or Bing, each is providing results based upon the text you have entered. While you can search on a single word in Google ("dogs"), most users try to narrow down their searches for better results ("Labrador vet specialists"). Broad searches are much, *much* harder to rank for, while narrow search phrases require some work but create more targeted traffic.

When selecting keywords for your site, think about how you would find your business or organization in the same way. If you sell designer earrings, the keyword "earrings" will be almost impossible to rank for on page one, due to the sheer competition for that term. But then how many users just search on "earrings" expecting useful results?

Chances are that "handmade diamond earrings" or "fashionable cheap earrings" will not only be easier to rank for, but visitors coming to your site will be searching for more specific terms, providing you with more valuable traffic. Visits or "hits" alone will not make your site successful - you want to attract quality traffic that has an interest in your niche topic. Site owners often struggle in determining their keyword phrases but there are a few simple exercises that can make the whole process easier.

First, think about how you would describe your business in one sentence to a total stranger. For example:

"'Where's the Beef?' is a steakhouse in downtown Houston featuring affordable aged steaks and live music."

From here, we can get some preliminary keywords and phrases: beef, steakhouse, houston, aged steak, live music - this is definitely an improvement on just "steakhouse" or "restaurant". We might have discovered from tip 8 that a local competitor is getting good traffic from the phrase "cajun ribeye" - so we would add this to the list if it were on our menu.

One you have a preliminary list of keywords, go to the Google AdWords Keyword Suggestion Tool at **https://adwords.google.com/select/KeywordToolExternal**.

All Categories

	All Categories
	Apparel
	Beauty & Personal Care
	Computers
	Consumer Electronics
	Family & Community
	Finance
	Food
	Gifts & Occasions
	Health
	Hobbies & Leisure
	Home & Garden
	Law & Government Products
	Media & Events

Contains
Sort: **Alphabetical** | Highest count

- ☑ All
- ☑ aged steak (9)
- ☑ houston (99)
- ☑ live music (3)
- ☑ steak (33)
- ☑ steak house (21)
- ☑ steakhouse (159)
- ☑ Miscellaneous terms (6)

Match Types
- ☑ Broad
- ☐ [Exact]
- ☐ "Phrase"

Help —

Why do search volume statistics vary between keyword tools?

How do I use the keyword tool to get keyword ideas and traffic estimates?

How do I get additional keyword ideas using categories or related terms?

Help Center

[Search help center] [Go]

Keyword ideas Sign in with your AdWords login information to see the full set of ideas for this search.   About this data ?

Download ▾   Sorted by Local Monthly Searches ▾   Views ▾

	Keyword		Competition	Global Monthly Searches	Local Monthly Searches	Local Search Trends
☐	houston	🔍		55,600,000	45,500,000	
☐	steakhouse	🔍		3,350,000	2,740,000	
☐	live music	🔍		2,240,000	1,500,000	
☐	steak house	🔍		1,220,000	823,000	
☐	steaks	🔍		1,000,000	823,000	
☐	outback steakhouse	🔍		823,000	673,000	
☐	prime rib	🔍		450,000	450,000	
☐	houston restaurant	🔍		301,000	301,000	
☐	restaurants houston	🔍		246,000	246,000	
☐	chop house	🔍		246,000	165,000	
☐	houston reservations	🔍		165,000	135,000	
☐	steak restaurants	🔍		165,000	135,000	
☐	steakhouses	🔍		165,000	110,000	
☐	houstons	🔍		110,000	110,000	
☐	steak restaurant	🔍		165,000	110,000	
☐	best steak	🔍		165,000	110,000	
☐	steakhouse menu	🔍		110,000	90,500	
☐	ruth chris steakhouse	🔍		90,500	90,500	
☐	morton's steakhouse	🔍		110,000	74,000	
☐	flemings steakhouse	🔍		49,500	49,500	
☐	prime steakhouse	🔍		49,500	40,500	
☐	new steakhouse	🔍		49,500	33,100	
☐	steak and seafood	🔍		40,500	33,100	
☐	steakhouse restaurant	🔍		40,500	27,100	
☐	best steakhouse	🔍		33,100	27,100	
☐	lonestar steakhouse	🔍		27,100	27,100	
☐	prime steak	🔍		33,100	27,100	
☐	sullivan's steakhouse	🔍		33,100	27,100	

The first pass of this exercise shows how broad phrases (single keywords and common phrases) have significant search volume, but high competition in Google AdWords. Above, there are 55.6 million monthly searches for the word "Houston", and the term is competed for aggressively in the AdWords market.

This isn't surprising, but nor is it particular useful - we need narrow, specific phrases that will deliver targeted traffic to our site, since users searching for Houston are not likely to be looking just for a steakhouse. So let's search again with the phrases **houston steakhouse**, **aged steak houston**, **cajun ribeye houston** and **best houston steakhouse**.

Search volume and competition for the phrases:

1. Houston steak-house
2. aged steak Houston
3. Cajun Ribeye Houston
5. best Houston steakhouse

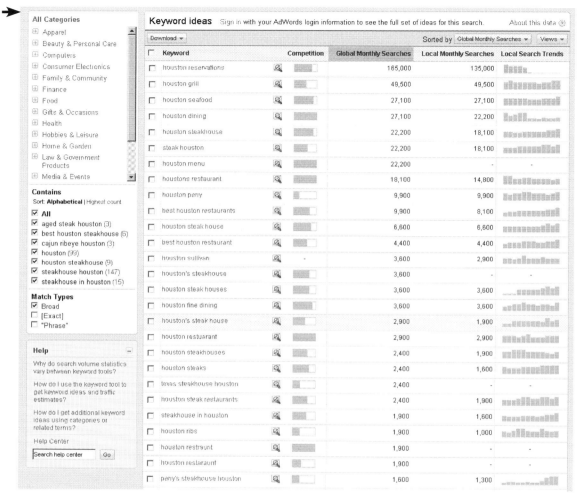

As the terms become narrower and more precise, the search volume falls from the millions, and the picture get clearer. "Aged steak Houston" receives less than 10 searches a month, so this term should be eliminated from our target keyword list.

But unexpectedly there are some terms showing in the list we had not previously considered, such as Houston grill, Houston reservations and Houston dining. Combined with the term Houston steakhouse, these have a global monthly search volume of 263,800 - which is a reasonable number for our site to target.

Next, we use Google to see how many web pages exist for each of these terms.

By entering each term into **http://google.com**, it's possible to see the number of web pages indexed for each phrase.

Enter each result in a spreadsheet, together with the monthly searches from the previous exercise, and you can see the phrases with the best search-to-competition ratio. In this case, "Houston reservations" and "Houston steakhouse" have only 22 and 41 pages per search respectively.

Search Term	Monthly Searches	Indexed Webpages	Ratio
Houston steakhouse	22,000	905,000	41
Houston dining	27,100	9,010,000	332
Houston reservations	165,000	3,650,000	22
Houston grill	49,500	5,090,000	103
aged steak Houston	10	163,000	16,300

As you keep testing different keyword phrases - 2, 3 and 4-word combinations - you will discover phrases that receive higher search volume, less page competition, and therefore a better chance for your pages to appear on page one when those terms are searched for.

Of course, Google is not the only search engine, and just because web pages exist for a phrase doesn't mean they are well designed or difficult to out-rank. Even if one term has more indexed pages than another, this isn't by itself a reason not to pursue it (especially if that phrase exactly describes what you do). But the battle is easier if there are fewer pages fighting for placement.

An automated approach

It's important to see how to do this manually but the idea generation is time-consuming enough to need automation to help speed things along. Keyword research is so important that I'd recommend using these tools to establish the phrases your site is going to rank for:

- **Keyword Discovery** is a fee-based service that brings all this data together, and more - including common spelling mistakes or variances, which can sometimes bring significant extra traffic (eg. "accomodation" as a basic typo, or "jewellery" as a British spelling of "jewelry").

- **Wordtracker** (which powers SEO Book's excellent Keyword Tool) checks across multiple engines to help find niche keyword phrases that offer the best opportunity for you to rank well.

Both services use data from hundreds of search engines and incorporate additional metrics that would be labor intensive to find manually. While I'd recommend the manual approach to help get your creativity flowing to help think about keywords and keyphrases, ultimately the competition for many keywords is so intense that almost everyone in the SEO business subscribes to services such as these.

10 **Avoid 'blackhat' SEO practices**

SEO tricks not only fail quickly, but will ultimately get your site removed from the indexes - maybe forever.

In the book's introduction, we talked about SEO's voodoo-like reputation. This is partly because there is more bad SEO advice out there than good, and this tip tries to deal with some of the problematic areas that will negatively affect your site's performance in search engines. I wish SEO were easier and more obvious - but it's not and the truth is that bad SEO practices can fatally affect your ability to create and maintain a presence on the web.

Is this so surprising? Web users are tired of spam and irrelevance - consequently, the search engines take the same zero-tolerance approach. What may seem an innocent way to leapfrog to the top of the search results will eventually lower your ranking at best and - at worst - have your site blacklisted. Once you're on the blacklist, there's no guarantee how long it will take to reinstate your position. Potentially, you may never appear on some search engines again.

Never use doorway pages

Doorway pages (also known as gateway pages) are optimized for one key term but are really designed to be gateways leading to different content. For example, a site might have pages designed for phrases such as "fixing printers", "printer advice" and "printer maintenance", all leading to a page about leasing office equipment, which is obviously unrelated. Essentially, this practice misleads the visitor for the sole purpose of building traffic for pages on a separate topic.

While this technique may gain traffic initially, it has a devastating impact on your SEO when engines realize what's going on. If you find yourself targeting phrases that are only very loosely linked to your real content, you're building a doorway page, and should immediately reconsider your strategy. This is arguably the number one blackhat SEO tactic.

> BMW famously had a doorway page in 2006 that resulted in their site being completely removed from Google's index (see http://blog.searchenginewatch.com/060202-121932). Using JavaScript, their site was able to separate human and spider visitors (cloaking), and target keywords not directly related to their products or services.

Using other people's trademarks

Large corporations and well known brands invest time and money into their trademarks: piggybacking them to promote your site is a bad idea. One of the classic 'black hat' techniques involves hijacking the success of established brands and trademarks to gain traffic.

By selecting a brand name as a keyword, knowing that the brand naturally gets a large number of hits (which is especially effective if the brand name is in the same industry), it's an attempt to avoid the real work of building your own brand and reputation. For example, using the keywords "American Airlines" and "Los Angeles" to promote an airport limousine business might be a quick way to generate hits, especially in a paid search campaign.

So why is this a bad idea? Essentially, however you look at it, this practice abuses trademarks and creates legal issues and potential liabilities. It's a black-hat strategy, designed to trick a search engine into believing your site is related to those terms, when in fact your limousine business has nothing to do with the airline.

- You might get away with it for a while, but ultimately search engines will discover your strategy and penalize your site.

- When the trademark owner alerts the engines with a Cease and Desist order, your site will likely be penalized for engaging in these practices.

- Large companies have lawyers - lots of them. Is it worth getting into a lengthy legal pursuit that you will probably lose?

There are many organizations - both large and small - targeting brands and trademarks they don't own, especially in the pay-per-click space. On the flip side, if you already own an established brand and find yourself a victim to this practice, there are services available that will monitor the trademark across the Internet on your behalf, and take the appropriate steps if abuse is discovered.

Given how many legitimate techniques there are to rank well, and the potential legal issues that can arise, my suggestion is to avoid this practice completely.

For more on doorway pages, see http://websearch.about.com/od/seononos/a/ doorways.htm, and to read about trademark bidding in paid search, go to http://www.wpromote.com/blog/internet-news/google-allows-trademark- biddinghysteria-ensures/.

Don't engage in cloaking

Cloaking is on the "Wanted List" for search engines - so don't do it. This is how it works: each visitor provides information about themselves when visiting a site (through the User-Agent HTTP header), which differentiates their hit from a search engine spider like GoogleBot. Using this information to work out 'real' visits from spiders, it's possible to provide different versions of the page, so that a search engine would see one thing and a real human another.

However you might justify it, this tactic is designed make a site behave differently depending on its human/spider audience. It's a bad strategy, especially since GoogleBot can just as easily appear as a browser agent and check the difference in the response. Basically, don't do it. Anything you do to separate search spiders and humans in terms of providing content will lead to lower ranking.

On the same topic, there are some other variants worth mentioning. Since search engines read HTML files and not the final rendered pages, there have been practices involving:

- Putting keywords on a page in the **same color as the background** making them invisible to a human but readable by a spider. This is called keyword spamming and while it worked 10 years ago will cause deranking now.

- **Using very small fonts** - such as point size 1 - to make keywords practically invisible to humans but visible to search engines. Again, it doesn't take much for spiders to realize that small fonts - as in indecipherably small fonts - are a trick.

- **Using CSS rules or JavaScript** to achieve the same thing: although this may seem repetitious, just because you move from one technology to another doesn't mean you won't get caught - and penalized. CSS makes it easier to cloak and I could enumerate the ways how spiders will find this but it's easier to simply recommend against doing this.

- **Using negative divs**: a div is a division tag in HTML, specifying the placement of a page element. Unscrupulous designers use these with negative X/Y coordinates to place content outside the visible page. The net effect is that search engines find the keywords in the text, yet the visitor does not see them. Again, this variant on cloaking should be avoided.

There is an argument for "good cloaking" saying that sometimes the technique is valid for cleansing URLs but spiders have become so good at parsing complex URLs that I don't see the need. Fundamentally, any practice intended to represent a page differently to a human versus a spider gets identified very quickly. Only the foolish or arrogantly brave even try this anymore - it's one of the easiest ways never to appear in search results again.

Keyword stuffing

Keyword stuffing is the practice of artificially adding strings of keywords all over your site, in the hope that the tedious repetition will fool search engines (if it doesn't drive visitors away first).

It's a golden oldie and no longer works - in fact, it will definitely work against you. The idea used to be that "keyword density" - the percentage of your page that are keywords - gave the indexes a good sense of the site's content, so the percentage could be gamed easily.

As you might imagine, spammers abused this very heavily, and now it has no positive effects on your ranking at all. See Google's advice at **http://www.google.com/support/webmasters/bin/answer. py?answer=66358** regarding this practice. These days, keyword stuffing seems to be the preserve of sites selling questionable health products and multi-level marketing scams, so it pays to keep better company and not copy this practice.

This tip only touches the surface of blackhat SEO techniques, which continuously evolve as the search engines upgrade their arsenal of weapons to fight back. Once again, if you find yourself engaged in practices that misrepresent your site's content somehow or don't seem entirely ethical, turn away from them immediately. And if an SEO company recommends a tactic that sounds too good to be true, it probably is.

Wikipedia has an excellent article on cloaking available at http://en.wikipedia. org/wiki/Cloaking. For the discussion on "good versus bad" cloaking, visit http:// searchengineland.com/good-cloaking-evil-cloaking-detection-10638.

SITE DESIGN

A website is a collection of web pages and although Google ranks individual pages rather than entire sites, how these pages are interconnected and managed has an impact on SEO. Many of the tips are common sense from the perspective of making the visitor experience as good as possible, but the vast majority are not implemented by a surprising number of sites.

Here we cover:

- Checking the load time of your site - slow sites drive visitors away.
- Validating your web pages to ensure compatibility across the broadest range of browsers.
- The pitfalls of Flash, frames and Ajax, and why these are bad for SEO.
- The benefits of using a content management system, and reasons for adding a blog to your site.
- Creating a sitemap for your web site, and ensuring your site's navigation is logical to visitors and search engine-friendly.

Good site design starts with the end user in mind and a good user experience directly translates to a good reputation in search engines.

11 Check the load time for your site

Patience is not a virtue on web pages. In fact, pages that load slowly drive visitors away, so test your site using free tools to find potential bottlenecks.

One frequently overlooked factor is that users have different ways to connect to the Internet, all of which have different speeds. If Internet connectivity is like the water supply, a T1 corporate connection is like a water main coming into the building, whereas dial-up can be like more like a shower with no pressure. Just because *your* connection is fast, don't assume your visitors experience anything like the same speed.

Using tools such as WebSiteOptimization.com's Analyzer (**http://websiteoptimization.com/services/analyze**), you can test your site for pages that are slow to load. This tool will examine a web page's assets (HTML, CSS, image and media files) and provide a 'Good vs. Bad' summary together with recommendations for improving speed. Some of the major causes for slow loading times include:

- **Large numbers of objects**: an object is anything your HTML links to. Many sites break images into smaller pieces to display decorative borders and visual effects, but doing so create more HTTP requests and slows down loading and rendering.

- **Large images**: pictures can be optimized for their display size on a web page, but it's common for their file sizes to be much larger than needed. Generating thumbnails and resampling for different resolutions can help keep these files small.

- **An excessive number of scripts**: JavaScript has become so common on web pages that many pages load a dozen scripts before starting, even if specific functions aren't used. Check to see if all the script is actually used on a page and if any script loading can be done at the end of the HTML (after the page is loaded). Also see if any of the files can be merged together and compressed.

Since cell phones are becoming a much more significant percentage of visitors for many sites, and 3G connections are slow compared to DSL, you could be driving away customers who come to your site on their iPhones or Androids. And it's not just cell phones - it's worth testing every page of your site from less dependable connections, such as airports, to ensure your pages load relatively quickly. Also, don't forget to test the load time after every major change on your site - it doesn't take much to transform a fast site to one that crawls along.

Analysis and Recommendations

- **TOTAL_HTML** - Congratulations, the total number of HTML files on this page (including the main HTML file) is 3 which most browsers can multithread. Minimizing HTTP requests is key for web site optimization. Y
- **TOTAL_OBJECTS** - Warning! The total number of objects on this page is 78 which by their number will dominate web page delay. Consider reducing this to a more reasonable number. Above 20 objects per page the overhead from dealing with the actual objects (description time and wait time) accounts for more than 80% of whole page latency. See Figure II-3: Relative distribution of latency components showing that object overhead dominates web page latency in Website Optimization Secrets for more details on how object overhead dominates web page latency. Combine, refine, and optimize your external objects. Replace graphic rollovers with CSS rollovers to speed display and minimize HTTP requests. Consider using CSS sprites to help consolidate decorative images. Using CSS techniques such as colored backgrounds, borders, or spacing instead of graphic techniques can reduce HTTP requests. Replace graphic text headers with CSS text headers to further reduce HTTP requests. Finally, consider optimizing parallel downloads by using different hostnames or a CDN to reduce object overhead.

Here are some other helpful tips to improve page load time:

- Use Pingdom (**http://pingdom.com**, shown below) to see how long every page element takes to load and determine potential bottlenecks.

- Always specify image heights and widths in your HTML: this boosts rendering time since the requesting browser doesn't have to wait and check the measurements from the downloaded image.

- For larger sites, consider a Content Delivery Network (CDN), which will host your content at third-party servers physically close to the visitor, dramatically improving load time.

- Implement caching on your server: the details will depend on your specific webserver technology but every major platform now offers a way of serving dynamic pages from a static cache, which helps with server load and download time.

- Host files on the same server: making calls to remote servers for images and other resources is almost always slower than hosting the files on the same server (with the exception of CDNs).

See Google's advice for improving page load time at http://code.google.com/speed/page-speed/docs/rtt.html#ParallelizeDownloads

Load time in seconds	URL	Size(KB)
1	oneuproar.com/	20
2	oneuproar.com/wp-content/libraries/OneUproar/script.js	10.3
3	oneuproar.com/wp-content/themes/OneUproar/style.css	21.6
4	...wp-content/plugins/cute-profiles/css/cute_profiles31.css?ver=1.0.1	8.7
5	...com/wp-content/plugins/wp-google-buzz/wp-google-buzz.js?ver=2.9.2	0.4
6	disqus.com/stylesheets/oneuproar/disqus.css?v=2.0	0.2
7	cdn.topsy.com/topsy.js?nt=topsyWidgetCreator	27.4
8	oneuproar.com/wp-content/plugins/wp-recaptcha/recaptcha.css	1.7
9	oneuproar.com/wp-content/uploads/One_Uproar_Ad_Graphic.png	69.6
10	oneuproar.com/wp-content/uploads/website_design.png	8.7
11	oneuproar.com/wp-content/uploads/social_media_icon.png	6.5

12 Validate your web pages

There are rules defining how HTML is used - if your site has poorly formed code, it may hinder the attempts of search engines to read and understand it.

Unlike a Word document or PDF, there's no concept of a fixed or accepted version of a webpage, which will change its appearance depending on operating system, browser type, browser version, installed fonts and user preferences. Good code can help bridge these differences and make a page look broadly the same all the way from Chrome on a Netbook to Safari on a Mac.

Search engine spiders and browsers are surprisingly resilient at reading bad code and making it work, but any errors become visible when comparing the same website in different browsers. The World Wide Web Consortium (W3C) is responsible for defining the standards behind HTML, and major browser developers such as Microsoft, Mozilla and Google adhere to these standards to ensure sites appear the same across browsers (and operating systems).

Still, websites are rampant with non-compliant HTML - you can test your site for compliance by visiting **http://validator.w3.org** and entering your site's URL. The validator will show errors and warnings, together with the likely causes and possible impact. You should note that the vast majority of websites don't pass validation, but it's still a worthy goal to aim for - being W3C-compliant gives your site the best chance of working in every browser,and being read accurately by every spider.

The web is becoming a standards-based environment: be a good Net Citizen by adhering to these standards, and both visitors and search engines will reward your site accordingly.

http://validator. w3.org *is the 'official' way to test your code for compliance to HTML standards.*

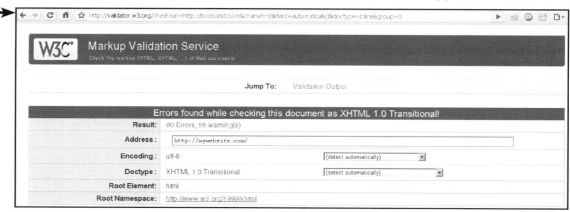

What is HTML/XHTML validation?

Web pages are usually written in HTML, XHTML and/or CSS, allowing the author to structure text, add media, specify appearance and style. Just like natural languages, these have their own grammar, vocabulary and syntax, and ideally every page follows the language's rules. However, just as human language can include spelling or grammar mistakes, documents based on markup languages may also contain errors.

In addition to the W3C tool on the previous page, there are other tools that test for code validation. In essence, these tools are code checkers and return any errors that may cause your website not to be displayed properly in a browser (and potentially not to be indexed by search engines). Not all errors are equally problematic, but it's best to fix errors in your syntax wherever possible.

Why is validation important?

Browsers try to display pages even if they're not valid HTML. Usually this means that the browser will try to make 'best guesses' about what the page is trying to do. The problem is that different browsers will make different guesses about the same code errors, so invalid pages will appear differently on different browsers. Generally speaking, you want your website to render identically independently of browser type, version or user operating system.

Browser Statistics Month by Month							
2010	**IE8**	**IE7**	**IE6**	**Firefox**	**Chrome**	**Safari**	**Opera**
February	14.7%	11.0%	9.6%	46.5%	11.6%	3.8%	2.1%
January	14.3%	11.7%	10.2%	46.3%	10.8%	3.7%	2.2%

←**http://www. w3schools.com/ browsers/brows-ers_stats.asp** *collects monthly statistics about which browsers are used most.*

Why does browser compatibility matter?

While Internet Explorer used to represent more than 80% of browser usage, surfers now use a broader selection of browsers (and different versions) to access web pages. A large portion of your web traffic likely comes from Mozilla Firefox, Google Chrome or Apple Safari, and code validation gives your site the best chance to render properly in each.

Another benefit of standards compliance is that new browsers and versions will be developed after the design and coding of your website is complete, and compliance ensures that your site will continue to function and appear as expected in the future.

13 Use Flash sparingly on your site

Flash brings real interactivity and media to websites. Unfortunately, it brings headaches for SEO since search engines can't see it.

This topic surfaces repeatedly in the SEO community, but it's still surprising to see how companies will invest $100,000 in a Flash website with the express intention of improving their search engine ranking. There are some really innovative Flash sites out there demonstrating real creativity, but while they will often be more interactive and, well, 'Flash' than traditional HTML/CSS sites, they will *always* rank lower in SERPs.

> 100% Flash websites don't rank well in search engines.

How GoogleBot sees a Flash site

The text and images of a Flash object are stored as a binary format so the animation you see in the final rendered version doesn't exist as 'readable' text in the containing HTML or FLV files. While Google and Adobe have both been getting better at making Flash movies more searchable, it's still the case that Flash sites rank poorly by comparison for 2 key reasons:

- **Google's sophistication** of looking beyond keywords to understand context is lost in metadata used to describe the movie content. A 100% Flash site may contain dozens of page with visible text content, but this will be summarized as a handful of keywords at the file level. In many cases, designers don't include the metadata at all.

- **Great designers** often don't know much about SEO (sorry, but it's true). In the example on the next page, which I screen-captured from an unnamed 100% Flash site, the TITLE attribute is the default value "Intro", and it's missing a META DESCRIPTION. A search engine has no chance of understanding that this site is for a national bar chain specializing in jazz and martinis.

At its most basic level, SEO is largely a text-driven business and robots can't read images and Flash well. Most Flash sites don't integrate well with Google Analytics (which is possible, but rarely done), making it difficult to collect metrics on where users are clicking and what pages within the site are the most popular. It's also not possible to bookmark individual pages, so the entry point into the site is always the same.

```
<HTML>
<HEAD>
<meta http-equiv=Content-Type content="text/html;  charset=ISO-8859-1">
<TITLE>intro</TITLE>
</HEAD>
<BODY bgcolor="#121212">
<center>
<!-- URL's used in the movie-->
<!-- text used in the movie-->
<!--er--><OBJECT classid="clsid:D27CDB6E-AE6D-11cf-96B8-444553540000"
 codebase="http://download.macromedia.com/pub/shockwave/cabs/flash/swflash.cab#version=6,0,0,0"
 WIDTH="700" HEIGHT="500" id="intro" ALIGN="">
 <PARAM NAME=movie VALUE="intro.swf"> <PARAM NAME=quality VALUE=high> <PARAM NAME=bgcolor VALUE=#121212>
<EMBED src="intro.swf" quality=high bgcolor=#121212 WIDTH="700" HEIGHT="500" NAME="intro" ALIGN=""
 TYPE="application/x-shockwave-flash" PLUGINSPAGE="http://www.macromedia.com/go/getflashplayer"></EMBED>
</OBJECT>
</center>
</BODY>
</HTML>
```

Search engines read the HTML pages to understand content, which is poorly represented in most 100% Flash sites.

Other problems with Flash

There are some cases where Flash elements on a page will improve the user experience and won't harm search engine rankings. Typically, these examples tend to be small and not central to the navigation or functionality of the page itself (such as interactive flight booking components on travel sites). Aside from the SEO problems from overusing Flash, there are myriad other issues:

- There's no guarantee that users have Flash installed - Flash is a plug-in not natively included with the majority of browsers. Relying on the presence of any plug-in is not a good strategy.

- It frequently results in much slower loading times, and therefore higher bounce rates. Flash movies can be large, and many users don't want to wait for a multi-megabyte movie to load.

- Many mobile devices don't support Flash (including the Apple iPhone and iPad).

- Initial design is more expensive and maintenance is usually very painful: it takes more time to code Flash than HTML/CSS, so typically costs more.

- It's difficult to make dynamic sites in Flash, compared with non-Flash, so Flash sites tend to be static. Also, RSS subscribers can't see the Flash content.

- It's easy to get carried away with overly-complicated animations and effects and completely lose the user. Most users want a fast unobtrusive way to reach your content rather than great design.

  While too much Flash is just plain bad for SEO, it can also just be a bad choice for creating a good user experience.

47

Avoiding Frames

While we're on the subject of web technologies to avoid, frames should be avoided at all costs. Introduced in the 1990s, the idea of frames was to break a single web page into panels in order to improve the speed of page navigation and simplify maintenance when new content needed to be added Frames are now a relic of the old web that unfortunately seem to stay with us - no serious major site uses frames anymore.

Framed pages are essentially an anathema to the concept of the web, which is fundamentally a large collection of pages joined together by links. Apart from printing problems, browser incompatibilities, bookmarking issues and glitches, search engines have trouble understanding the relationship between frames and pages. Anything that's bad for search engine spiders is bad for SEO, in addition to the fact they create a terrible user experience for the most part.

I've not heard a good argument for frames in a long time, and my suspicion is that they will disappear altogether with the rise of the mobile web. There is an excellent page called The World's Worst Website that demonstrates, among other things, frames as a major offender in usability.

Visit the self-proclaimed World's Worst Website at **http://www.angelfire.com/super/badwebs.**

The SEO limitations of AJAX

AJAX - or Asynchronous JavaScript - has the ability to deliver new content to a web page without reloading the entire page, so has become the underlying technology for extremely responsive and application-like pages such as Gmail and Google Maps. AJAX has the ability to massively improve the user experience on a web page but can be a obstacle for SEO if not implemented judiciously.

The core problem is that search engine spiders examine the HTML on your web pages but don't actually run AJAX requests. Consequently, any content that's dynamically provided as a result will not get indexed in the same way as regular text or images. Like Flash, AJAX is an SEO issue when it's overused, since everything loads under a single URL and it disrupts classic browser navigation.

Current best practices suggest that AJAX should be used for elements that will not affect ranking - such as user logins, showing random client testimonials, managing member areas and so forth. It's wise to avoid it for site navigation or large portions of content retrieval, otherwise you run the risk of search engines failing to crawl and index your content completely. I expect this will change in the future given the promising future that AJAX has, but the best SEO advice for now is to use it sparingly and away from keyword-sensitive content.

To read more about AJAX and SEO, visit http://www.searchenginejournal.com/ seo-for-ajax/19138.

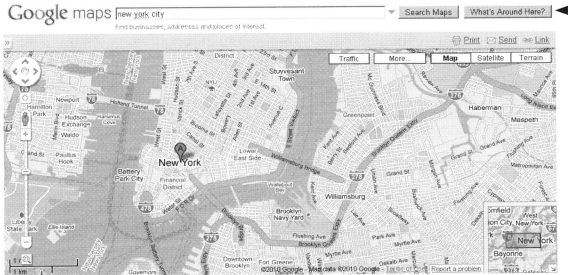

Google Maps is one of the most famous AJAX applications on the web.

a Content Management System

d CMS will manage your layout, content, data-
es and user interaction - if you are building a new
ce in 2010 and beyond, chances are you need a CMS.

SEO is about content - not just any old content, but changing and dynamic content that is timely and relevant. This means that the old days of 5-page static websites simply don't rank well anymore (unless they're for very niche, uncompetitive keyword phrases), and you need to be able to create, delete and update pages regularly without going back to your web designer.

There's no easier way to do this than using a Content Management System, such as WordPress, Drupal or Joomla (there are many others but these are all free and well supported). The CMS acts as a container for everything on your site, and manages much of the mundane housekeeping that otherwise you would have to deal with. By and large, CMS-driven sites are inherently friendly to search engines and handle the technical side of serving pages, and - not surprisingly - managing content.

There are web design companies who shy away from these technologies because they simplify the web design process (resulting in less work!) but don't be discouraged - just because it reduces their fees doesn't make it bad choice for your website. And in choosing a CMS, you're keeping good company: content-rich sites such as CNN, the New York Times, WSJ.com and MTV.com are all based upon CMS platforms. These off-the-shelf solutions will handle your site more easily and effectively than a platform you build from scratch.

Implementing a CMS is beyond the scope of this book, but in general the key points are:

- Most popular CMS platforms are free (and open source) and have lively communities of plugins, themes and extensions, enabling your site to add new functionality easily. My personal favorite for ease-of-use is WordPress, which offers a one-click install on many web hosts.

- They're theme-driven, meaning pages are served based upon a template that creates them dynamically depending on content. When you add a new page to your site, the CMS simply uses the theme to build the page - with no additional programming needed. If you want to change the theme, the whole site receives the new look instantly (rather than changing page-by-page).

- These systems are mature, stable and robust: if you want a site that can withstand millions of visitors and page views and not crash, a CMS is surely the way to go.

An example: WordPress and SEO

In terms of number of users, WordPress is the most popular of the free CMS platforms available.

The major SEO benefit is simple: since there's no need for programming knowledge or HTML to manage pages, your time and design efforts can be focused on creating content rather than dealing with technicalities. New, original, relevant content is at the heart of SEO - here are some of the benefits:

- If you have several content producers in your organization, WordPress handles multiple users, content revision and media, making it more like editing a document in a word processor than coding for web pages.

- WordPress' famed "All-in-One SEO" plug-in by Michael Torbert manages some of the more mechanical on-page SEO factors in a more automated fashion (**http://wordpress.org/extend/plugins/all-in-one-seo-pack/installation**).

- There are many plug-ins to increase user interaction, such as PollDaddy and GD Star Rating, as well as user forums and social media integration. Anything that engages your user, driving links and participation, will help SEO.

Additionally, to maximize the SEO effect of running a WordPress installation:

- Change the permalink structure to "**/%postname%/**" to embed your title into the URL of each page and post.

- Use categories and tags to emphasize keywords on posts and provide a topical structure for archives. Add the categories widget to your design, so users can drill-down through posts by using your chosen keywords.

- Keep your posts on-topic and relevant: a site that focuses on topics that are closely related will be more popular with visitors and search engines than one that changes subject constantly.

- Reduce your bounce rate (the percentage of visitors who view one page on your site before leaving) by adding the "Show Related Posts" plug-ins. This helps provide relevant outbound links on each page.

- Keep your WordPress installation up to date, and use the .htaccess files on your server to restrict administrative access and keep security problems at bay (see tip 27).

- Getting your site hijacked by spammers can get your site delisted from the engines, so ensure you have secure passwords to prevent brute-force attacks on your admin account.

The WordPress platform provides a solid and extendable basis for your website, providing the best starting point for SEO from a technical perspective.

15 Add a blog to your site

Blogs are like a visitor magnet for your site. They're easy to set-up, popular and yet most sites don't have one. If you want visitors, you need a blog!

We're back to content again, and there's no better or easier way to generate timely and relevant content than to add a blog. Organizational blogs give businesses a way to connect with visitors in a unique way and a good blog will boost visitor numbers, encourage repeat visits and send your pages marching up the search result rankings.

Why is this?

- **Expertise**: blogs allow you to talk about topics in your industry or field. If you are a locksmith, discuss the benefits of new locks on the market. If you are a restaurant, post exciting recipes for readers to try. If the content is good, visitors will send the links to other people, or recommend the posts on social media sites such as Digg, StumbleUpon and Twitter.

- **Linkability**: blog posts are among the most commonly hyper-linked pages on the web. This matters since inbound links are vital to SEO and they can otherwise be surprisingly hard to get. If you have quality blog posts that readers like and link to, you are on your way to SEO stardom.

- **Interactivity**: many blogging platforms provide interactive elements such as user comments, ratings and votes. Visitors want to be able to provide feedback on your site so creating a dialog through blog content is a good way to introduce visitors to your site. Regular visitors who like your site eventually become regular customer who like your business.

- **Dialog**: visitors have tuned out to the classic one-way marketing pitches and product spiels. They don't believe your claims, and want authenticity in the messages your company provides. Blogs provide a way to provide a more interesting two-way conversation with your audience.

Blogs are no longer the casual user diary or amateur journalism that they used to be, and have become credible sources of news and information for many Internet users. Adding a blog is technically very easy (especially if you're using a CMS) and one can be added to a sub-domain or directory on your site (eg. **http://blog.mycompany.com** or **http://mycompany.com/blog**).

> Make sure that if you have a hosted blog the content is either redirected as above, or you purchase a domain name, otherwise the SEO benefit will stay with the hosting company and not your own site.

Blogging 101

There's nothing to say that blogging shouldn't be fun, but there are some basic unwritten rules that have developed over time and will get you the best reputation and exposure if you follow:

- **Stay on topic**: restrict your blog posts to industry or professional areas and absolutely avoid rants about the government, politics, movies or anything else that strays off topic (and potentially alienates your readers). A great example of a corporate blog is **http://www.dell.com/blog**.

- **Be controversial and challenging** (but not mean or difficult): while it's initially easier to get traffic by being confrontational, you'll build a higher quality audience by challenging the status quo or developing new ideas. A chef with a new way to cook turkey is more interesting than hearing about a tried and tested method.

- **Focus on your title**: your title will be the biggest driver of traffic - good titles attract clicks. Spend as much time thinking about your (keyword-heavy) title as you do writing the blog post.

- **Write lists**: top 10 lists have become extremely popular in the blogosphere. If you can break your post into a bullet-point list of items, it will often attract more interest.

- **Use the title formula**: this may seem corny, but one suggested title formula goes: "X adjective noun to Keyword Phrase (and Keyword Phrase)". This means instead of "Energy savings tips for your house" use "10 Simple Ways to Save Energy and Cut Your Bills".

- **Be brief**: writing somewhere between 250 and 500 words for your blog post seems to be ideal for balancing quality content length (for search engines) and attention span (for humans). If you find yourself going to thousands of words, break up your post into smaller topics.

- **Comment and link to other blogs**: find blogs dealing with similar topics, leave comments and reference their pieces in your writing. Blog owners enjoy debate and inclusion, and they'll most likely reciprocate the favor.

- **Write regularly**: search engines reward new content with priority ranking, but visitors love new content and come back to read more. If you set the expectation that you'll publish one quality blog post a week, you have to keep up that commitment. Many people start blogging daily and quickly find the frequency drops to once a week or worse - find a comfortable interval that you can maintain for the long term.

When it comes to content, adding a blog to your site is one of the most valuable steps you can take to improve your online reputation. It can be fun (and frustrating) but your patience and consistency will make you stand head and shoulders above competing sites and can give you a major SEO boost in the long run.

When you update a regular web page, search engines can take days or weeks to pick up the new content and include it in the index. Search engines have a natural bias towards blog content, due to their need to provide timely results, so blog content tends to be picked up significantly more quickly. You can inform search engines and blog directories of new content using Pingomatic (**http://pingo-matic.com**) which will automatically tell a couple of dozen services on your behalf.

Handling comments

Since comments are enabled on most blogs, responding to feedback is an important part of blog maintenance. Comments largely fall into the following categories:

- **Positive and constructive feedback**: when visitors appreciate the value of your content, they'll let you know. It's important to respond in the comment thread to indicate you've read their response and valued the time it took them to write something on your page. Good feedback can also provide ideas for future posts, and if you start to build a relationship with this audience may also be a good place to find "guest bloggers" for your own blog.

- **Negative feedback**: if an unhappy customer uses your blog to vent frustration with your service, use this as an opportunity to address their concerns and win back their support. Don't simply delete the comment or be defensive - treat the complaint the same way you would if the person called or wrote you.

- **Trolling**: unfortunately, the Internet has a fair population of people trying to draw attention to themselves by being offensive and obnoxious. When you detect this, simply delete their comments. Depending upon which blogging software you use, you can optionally block the IP addresses of repeat offenders.

- **Spam**: comment spam is a huge problem on blogs, but there are some easy ways to counteract it by implementing Disqus or ReCAPTCHA. Both of these are designed to block automated spam by requiring user profiles or reading tests that can usually only be performed by humans. While some spam always seems to get through, whenever you find spam, simply delete it.

- **Pingbacks and trackbacks**: although these usually appear as comments, they're essentially pointers to where another site has referenced your content. These can be useful for finding where web users are engaging your content, and can also help develop an audience.

Although managing comments can be time-consuming, depending on the popularity of your blog, it's an essential part of building a following. The worst thing you can do (apart from disabling comments entirely) is to ignore responses - apart from allowing a site to get overrun with spam, users eventually stop providing feedback if they're not acknowledged.

RSS: It's Really Simple (Syndication!)

Indicate your site is RSS-ready by displaying the RSS icon

RSS allows visitors to subscribe to your content without having to visit your site directly. It makes it easier to follow your content on their terms.

If you follow large numbers of websites or access the web on mobile devices regularly, RSS Readers allow you to stay on top of changing content by alerting you of changes. One popular reader is Google Reader (**http://reader.google.com**, shown below), where users can add all the sites and feeds they intend to follow, and the tool manages the rest.

By maintaining a subscription to your site through the reader, the user never has to visit your site directly to see the new content. Your updates become aggregated with the updates of other feeds, creating a one-stop shop for everything that's new. One of the useful benefits is that in some RSS readers, subscribers can share interesting feeds with each other - another way for your site to gather new visitors using the network of existing users.

If you're using a CMS then RSS is likely built in, but for proprietary sites you'll need a web developer to add RSS functionality for you. Given the growing popularity of RSS and the ease in which it can be added to a website, this is a great way to extend your site's reach.

Google Reader is one of the many RSS feed aggregators available. An RSS feed can be shown in any webpage, widget or application that understands RSS.

16 **Use meaningful filenames**

Always embed descriptive phrases and keywords into your pages and resources.

On a desktop PC or network, data is stored in a tree-like structure that help the system and user locate the files they need. You might well be used to storing your year-end budget in a file called 2010 Year End Budget.xls in a directory called C:\Files\MyCompany\Accounting.

Web servers work exactly the same way and all the pages on a site resolve to a filename on a server somewhere. For example, the file **http://oneuproar.com/50-seo-tips/recommended-hosting-providers.html** resolves to a file that lives in the directory /public_html/50-seo-tips called recommended-hosting-providers.html. For all intents and purposes, the http:// at the beginning is just like a drive letter (and all the forward slashes are like backslashes).

Since the filename is part of the public URL visible on the Internet, and search engines assume that filenames provide some meaningful guide to the content of the file, it pays to provide good descriptions in the filename. A good description should be accurate and include keywords where appropriate, but not repetition of the domain name. Filenames can consist of letters, numbers and certain punctuation such as dashes and underscores:

- There is a debate about whether uppercase or lowercase is preferred (such as SEO-tips.html or seo-tips.html). It's arguably better to keep all directory names and filenames in lowercase, not least because users have become accustomed to URLs being lowercase. Also, depending on your server setup, URLs can be case-sensitive so if you use confusing capitalization it can result in a 404 error (i.e. the file's missing).

- Spaces aren't allowed in URLs and aren't human-friendly when converted - for example, the filename *SEO tips.html* would appear as SEO%20tips.html in the URL. Don't use spaces in your filenames, even though you can use these on desktop operating systems.

- For technical reasons there is a bias towards dashes rather than underscores, so blue-widgets.html is preferred to blue_widgets.html (and both are better than bluewidgets.html, since it's easier to decipher the individual words).

The directory structure can be used to reinforce keywords in the content, but only use this where appropriate, such as:

- http://mysportsoutlet.com/products/shoes/nike-air.html

- http://myrestaurant.com/breakfast/american-breakfast.html
- http://mysite.com/images/baseball-cap.html

Nesting content several directories deep is considered spammy - just as having unnecessarily keyword-laden files raises alarm bells, so the following examples would not be good for SEO:

- http://myshoesite.com/running/shoes/sports/athletic/marathon/new-york/athletic-running-sports-shoes.html
- http://best-cheapest-air-flights.com/ best-cheapest-air-flights.com/ best-cheapest/air-flights/travel/air/cheap/best-cheapest-air-flights.html

If these seem like ridiculous examples, let me assure you there are plenty of sites using keyword spamming - as a human, it's not hard to spot, and even the search engine spiders can see what they're trying to do. Ideally, a site's directory structure should be sensible and human-friendly, and designed to help locate content. In terms of length, your filenames should be as short as they can be while conveying what they contain effectively.

As an aside, your URL file extension doesn't matter: you can use .html, .htm, .asp, .php, etc. and it won't make a difference from an SEO perspective. You should aim to be consistent, however, so if you use .htm extensions, don't switch to .html half way through your site.

URLs to avoid

Most e-commerce sites depend on a database to store product information and session IDs to track visitors, so often the URLs are structured to pass data back and forth and retain state rather than be visitor- or SEO-friendly, such as **http://mycompany.com/jp/product/B0039XZ3PW/ref=s9_ simh_gw_ p65_i1?&pf_rd_i=507846**.

These URLs contain parameters for the content management system to keep track of what's happening, but don't do much for SEO or real visitors. Also, since these parameters may be dynamic, the URL may change whenever a new session ID is established (and stop working when a session expires), so the URLs become invalid when there's a change in state.

Search engines have a hard time navigating sites that use dynamic and multiple parameters in the URL, basically because the idea that a URL represents a stateless resource somewhere on the web starts to break down. In some cases, they can cause duplicate content problems (see tip 28) since the same series of URLs can point to the same page. Overall, it's better to hide the design and inner workings of your site under the hood, and keep the URLs simple.

17 **Think about the mobile audience**

Mobile is getting more important and while there are different challenges to creating a following, there is still a first-mover advantage for many businesses.

Most web pages are accessed using desktop or laptop computers (see **http://marketshare.hitslink. com/report.aspx?qprid=0** for a comparison of popular browsers) and mobile phones remain a small minority of surfing devices, though this is rapidly changing. Use Google Analytics (tip 42) to check how much of your traffic comes from mobile - if it's significant, there are three areas you can focus on to improve the mobile user's experience.

Providing a mobile-friendly site

Maximizing for small screen size

If you've ever loaded a regular web page on a mobile device, you probably know it can be difficult to navigate due to the screen size being considerably smaller than a regular monitor. Designing the view to fit the narrower width allows your visitors to quickly find what they need without scrolling around. This also has an influence on the font sizes your site uses, together with the amount of content per page - on mobile, less is more. See how your site appears on an iPhone at **http://testiphone.com** (shown right).

Working with less bandwidth

Right now, 3G connections are considerably slower than DSL at home or the T1 lines in many businesses. Clunky, bandwidth-hungry sites can load with no noticeable slowness through a larger pipe but are agonizingly slow when pulled through the air on mobile.

The best mobile sites optimize for the worst-case bandwidth scenario and still provide a timely response on a poor connection. On mobile, any page more than 20K in size can appear sluggish and unresponsive when the network connection is poor.

> The iPhone and many other mobile devices don't support Flash - 100% Flash sites will be invisible on these devices until HTML alternatives are set up.

Left: this site on an iPhone is too wide to view comfortably, so the visitor has to scroll to read all the content. Check how your site appears on an iPhone at **http://testiphone.com**.

Right: this site uses a mobile-specific template to optimize the screen size and page load time. WPtouch is a plug-in for the WordPress platform.

Mobile-specific template

Your site receives the user agent type from an incoming HTTP request, so it's possible to change the content returned depending on whether the request is from a desktop or mobile browser. You can serve one version of the site to a desktop browser, and another to a mobile. For any proprietary site, it involves some programming and design work to make this happen seamlessly.

If you're using a CMS platform, many now have plug-ins that can automate a large portion of the work. For example, WordPress has the WPtouch plug-in that automatically converts your pages into lightweight mobile-ready layouts with no additional programming needed.

The benefit of this approach is that your design can be optimized for both desktop and mobile browsers without compromising performance for either.

Location as an SEO factor

Arguably the biggest change as mobile arrives is location - before, we only knew a visitor's location very coarsely, but now it's possible to pinpoint their position precisely through GPS.

Not only does this allow content and search to be optimized very specifically (who wants a pizza delivery in Brooklyn when their phone is on the Upper West Side?) but also means user behavior is different on mobile devices and expectations can be different:

- For businesses, information such as opening hours, parking and contact details needs to be more accessible.

- Special offers and time-sensitive information is often more important to the mobile user, who is searching for your business based upon his or her needs *right now*.

- Using media is more common so photos and video are useful to the mobile visitor - moreover, the ability to post user-generated media content can provide higher levels of engagement.

A business' profile on FourSquare, showing the number of visitors, check-ins, user tips and the current Foursquare Mayor.

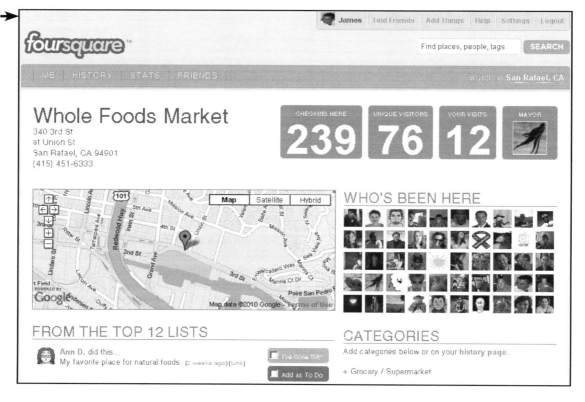

Location-driven sites and mobile apps

Some third-party sites have invested heavily in location-specific applications and web interfaces - depending on your business, ensure your business listing on these services is up-to-date:

- **Yelp.com**: their mobile applications find businesses based upon the user's current phone location, and users can then add photos and reviews directly from their device. Add your business to their directory for free at **http://www.yelp.com/business**.

- **Foursquare** (shown left) combines a local business directory with a competitive game - members "check-in" at venues when they're within a couple of hundred feet, and the person who has visited the business most often becomes the Mayor. Businesses then have the choice of offering their Mayors perks to help fuel the competition. Add your venue to Foursquare at **http://foursquare.com/add_venue**.

- **Gowalla** is also a location-based travel game that rewards visitors for checking in at locations. You have to add your business using the mobile application rather than the website (**http://gowalla.com**).

- **Google Maps** contains a profile of business, merging data across Internet sources with Google's street view imagery. Since Maps powers local search and GPS navigation on Android phones, completing your profile will make your business and site more visible to mobile users (see tip 38 on building your Google Local Business Center profile).

For larger businesses, developing their own mobile applications provides a compelling way to 'lock-in' the mobile audience. Amazon.com, Zillow, USAA and HotelsByMe.com have all successfully tailored their content for mobile devices, and there is a first-mover opportunity for businesses solving location-specific problems using apps.

The question of serving mobile-specific content on your website depends upon your audience - for many business and organizations, it isn't yet an issue, and probably isn't worth the development time. But keep watching mobile usage statistics through your Google Analytics account - as the popularity of iPhones, Androids and Blackberries continue to surge, in a couple of years it may no longer be an option to leave the mobile community out in the cold.

For some ideas on how location will impact SEO, visit http://blog.hubspot.com/blog/tabid/6307/bid/5689/3-Ways-Location-Will-Change-SEO.aspx.

18 Write for users first, engines second

Design content to keep visitors engaged on your site and search engines will rank you accordingly.

Your website is not an island blasting out its marketing message 24/7 - at least it shouldn't be. In real life, your company exists as an entity in a real location, with real regular customers, all of which have their own interests and concerns. On the web, your community is slightly different since its members are almost certainly more geographically dispersed, but they do have still have issues, problems and ideas that you can engage in. Your goal must be to create content that gets involved with these conversations that are happening with your online audience.

The objective of search engines is simple - regardless of the differences in their algorithms for crawling and indexing sites, they all strive to answer user queries in the shortest time possible, and ensure the most relevant and highest quality sites appear at the top of the results. If you create web pages that do both, search engines will reward you with the ultimate accolade of number one placement.

Many of the tips in this book are technical in nature or try to improve your exposure by maximizing different content channels, or getting in front of your potential audience in ways other than just pushing a site on the web. These tips are vital in beating the competition out of the top spot, but you won't get very far unless you think beyond the technology and address the needs of your visitors to keep them coming back.

Popular sites consider content, style and design all together to keep visitors returning:

- **Write emotively**: your content should reveal the personality of your product or service, and there's nothing wrong with being funny or having a point of view.

- **Use short sentences**: reading on screens is difficult. True. But there's also a trend towards shorter sentences. They're less confusing.

- **Be consistent**: make the site navigation, style and design consistent and obvious as the visitor moves between pages (see tip 19).

- **Don't forget the call to action**: while your site should not be one long sales pitch, don't be afraid to remind the visitor to call you, sign-up or do whatever it is that you need.

- **Avoid eyesores**: animated GIFs, "marquee" text animation, garish colors - basically, anything you would have seen on websites in 1996.

In SEO, site design is almost always discussed from a technical or HTML perspective, but actually good design is primarily for humans rather than search engine spiders. Web design, like any creative endeavor, can benefit greatly from the expertise of a design firm.

8 Things Every Business Site Needs

These are things we all expect in other people's sites but frequently forget when it comes to our own:

- **Contact information**: your phone number and email need to appear on every page of your site. Even now, most people prefer to pick up a phone, and making them hunt for your phone number is a surefire way to deter them.

- **Location**: where are you? Include an embedded Google Map, directions if necessary and a picture of your property. It looks suspicious to hide this information.

- **Your opening hours**: for any business that customers have to visit, your opening hours should be current and prominently visible throughout your site. Include holiday closures, extended hours and any other pertinent information.

- **Your picture and biography**: while many people shy away from putting their picture online, it creates a sense of legitimacy and trust if you expect your visitors to buy things from you. Transactions are the by-product of healthy relationships, so build your relationships first.

- **A summary of your products or services**: it should be instantly obvious from any page on your site what your business is and does, yet so many sites having strange domain names, overly artistic design or poor layout that it's a struggle for the average visitor to guess what's going on.

- **Privacy policy and terms of use**: did you know your web server collects personal data from your visitors such as their IP address? Did *they* know you're collecting that? This has nothing to do with SEO and everything to do with being transparent (and not getting sued).

- **Copyright notice**: every one of your web pages belongs to you - it's important to make this point clearly on the footer of every page. Incidentally, if you want to include the year in the notice, on any server technology it's just a one-line piece of code to keep the year current.

- **Search box**: Google site search can be installed on any site in seconds and provides the user with the familiar iconic box that will find the page they need. It's also easy to implement your own search mechanism, but the Google tool is so simple and effective, why reinvent the wheel?

For a comprehensive list of web page design errors to avoid, visit http://www.webpagesthatsuck.com.

19 Site navigation

Poor navigation is one of the major reasons that visitors leave sites and pages don't get indexed.

How many times have you been on a website and not been able to find pages that you thought should be obvious? Websites by their very nature are a collection of pages linked together by a navigation system and when that system is poorly designed, it's much like a road system with poor signs and unexpected turns - the visitor (or driver) ends up in the wrong place, misses their turn and gets frustrated. Web usability author Steve Krug puts it elegantly in his book titled *Don't Make Me Think* when he observes that poor navigation makes us stop and think, whereas well designed navigation is almost invisible.

Examples of poor navigation are not hard to find, and while it's relatively rare to see bad navigation built to a brand new site, it seems to develop and deteriorate as more content and pages are added without any thought to the overall page-to-page linking. Frustration is a major reason why users give up on websites, so it's essential to maintain obvious navigation even as your site gets larger.

Website owners often imagine that everyone will be coming in through the front door - otherwise known as the home page (e.g. **http://mysite.com**) - but site statistics tend to prove otherwise. While the bulk of your traffic will point to the top-level domain when the site is first launched, as you gather more inbound links and increase your online reputation, a growing percentage of hits will be targeted to individual pages nested in your site.

Keep in mind some of the most popular ways that users find your web pages:

- **Search engine results** often send traffic to the page in your site that's most relevant for the user's search query, rather than the top-level home page. Don't leave those users stranded with nowhere to go, or your bounce rates will be sky-high.

- **PPC landing pages**: if you're using paid ads, every ad should be arriving on its own unique keyword-rich landing page. Each one of those needs to include the site's ordinary navigation or your conversion rates after you paid for the click will be much lower.

- **Bookmarked URLs** that visitors email or Tweet to each other. When users click these URLs, they must show exactly the same content that the sender was shown, otherwise there's no benefit to sending the link in the first place.

Features of Bad Navigation

While it's hard to define exactly what bad navigation is, you know when you see it. Inspecting a range of bad sites, I believe that these characteristics should be avoided:

- **Orphaned pages**, where you have to arrive there by some external or illogical link, and cannot get back without searching your browser history.

- **Poorly named pages**: for example, while it may seem unique or clever to rename the 'Contact' page 'Reach Out' or 'Talk to us', it isn't intuitive. Visitors are used to seeing 'Contact' in the page name so there's no real benefit in not meeting their expectations.

- **Lack of links**: pages that discuss a product sold on the site, but don't show how to order it; or pages that mention a topic of interest previously discussed with no way to get back to the topic.

- **Pages with no navigation** because the site presumes that everyone reaches a page through their structure (without landing through a search engine result), and the visitor arrives with no way to find the main entry point - or any other major page - on the site.

- **Structure designed for a company** or industry, not reflecting terminology a customer would use. This is more common in technical businesses but leaves the visitor completely confused.

- **Changing layouts** with menus jumping around from page to page, so the user can't predict where items will be on the page.

- **Requiring registration** before viewing a page. While it's great to build site membership and encourage visitors to register, requiring this up-front by either denying access or showing an annoying pop-up light box will turn people away. I see this on a growing number of media sites, which is incredibly counter-productive given the competitiveness of their market.

- **Opening every link** in a new window. While many designers say that you should never direct your users away from your site, I believe that opening windows without the user's consent can be irritating. Also, depending upon the browser's security settings, the link may never open, leading the user to believe your site is broken.

- **Image-based or JavaScript-driven menus**, which can work when designed well, but frequently make the text hard to read or find. Generally, apart from the fact that search engines cannot read graphics, image-based menus take longer for visitors to absorb and understand. As for JavaScript, if you want to use it you must provide alternative navigation for users that have this disabled and ensure the text and links are visible to search engines outside the JavaScript code.

All of these problems stem from the same basic mistake: getting in the way of the user and preventing the exploration of your content.

Features of good navigation

It's important to scour the Internet for both major sites and competitors and see what works (or doesn't) in their navigation. Best practices are starting to appear:

- **Navigation placement** should be at the top or left or your page. Placing navigation controls on the right can be problematic given screen-width issues, and may not be visible to users with lower screen resolutions.

- **Navigation animation** should be minimal. If users must hover over categories to make sub-categories appear (as in a regular desktop application), set the hover delay to zero and think twice before using animation that slows down the visitor.

- **Limit the top-level menu** to around 5-8 items - cramming a dozen or more top-level links offsets the benefit of structured navigation.

- **Show the current page** and use 'bread crumbs': if a page is nested two or three levels deep, state this clearly at the top using "Home > Category > Sub-category > This Page", where each level is a hyperlink that can jump back to any previous level.

- **Clear page names** and obvious links aid navigation - using well-named anchor text (see tip 29) isn't just a good SEO tactic, it also gives the visitor a clear indication if the link is worth following.

- **Add navigation** on the page footer including at least the basic links, so that users don't have to scroll back the top to get around your site. A growing number of sites are using more elaborate footer menus that link to popular content and clearly delineate the end of the page.

- **Maintain the same layout** through-out your site. It's surprisingly how many sites hide navigation on some pages or - possibly worse - change the tab order depending on the page.

- **Respect the browser** controls so that Back, Forward and Refresh buttons work as expected. "Back" is the second most popular navigational feature after hyperlinks. It's tremendously annoying to visitors when session state is lost or any sort of multi-step form is broken just by using native browser controls.

Using Google Analytics you can quickly see which pages are the most popular, and which hardly get used. If a top-level page is rarely visited, demote that page in order to funnel more attention to the pages that visitors want to visit. For example, your Privacy Policy page is important but will be ignored by most users, so add the link on the footer menu rather than the top.

For more ideas, see Steve Krug's two books on website usability: Don't Make Me Think and Rocket Surgery Made Easy.

A good site hierarchy should reflect the relationship between all the pages, and provide obvious navigation.

Building your hierarchy

On most websites, pages are logically nested in some of tree-like hierarchy, all stemming from the main home page. The navigation should reflect this natural order, with menu clearly delineating different topics of the site, and offering drill-down menus where the tree is more than 2 levels deep.

One SEO rule of thumb is that pages should be no more than two clicks away from the home page - this is true to an extent, but it's probably more useful to say that pages shouldn't be any deeper in the tree than they have to be. If you have a product catalog with dozens of nested subcategories, you should rethink the structure of the product categorization before translating that into an unworkable menu system.

If you have a range of products available, split the content so one page represents a single product, rather than listing everything on a single page. Showing multiple products dilutes SEO since they can often represent multiple keyword phrases. It pays to show 250-1,000 words per page - if you have more than 1,000 words, consider splitting up the content into several pages.

While the structure will come to resemble a tree, such as the one shown above, ensure that links appear on every page for user account management, shopping carts, contact information, logging out and other popular pages and tasks. Also ensure that these links are shown in the same place, so your visitors know where to find these functions.

20 Generate a site map file

A sitemap is like a table of contents for your site and can help search engines understand the structure.

Sitemaps allow website owners to give search engines a complete listing of all their web pages, together with additional data that may not be included in the pages themselves (called metadata). This additional data includes information such as how often the page is updated and its importance relative to other pages on the site.

Once a sitemap is created, it's submitted to the major search engines for their consideration, either using automated tools or manual submission through Google Webmaster Tools, Yahoo! Site Explorer or Bing. While there's no guarantee regarding whether it will be used, it can typically help search engine spiders in understand the structure of the whole site.

The sitemap itself is an XML file and can provide additional benefit for sites that have web pages that are not reachable through internal links or navigation (see the previous tip on good navigation practices). Additionally, pages with extensive Ajax or Flash elements that would not normally be handled well by search engines can benefit from sitemap metadata.

It's important to realize that sitemaps do not replace the proprietary mechanisms used by search engine spiders, nor do they influence their ranking methodologies. In a site with a good navigation system and no orphaned pages (those without links from other pages on the web), a site map may provide only minor benefit. As with so many SEO techniques, however, creating a sitemap is free and submission is easy, so there's no harm in using this method.

Creating and submitting the sitemap file

The easiest way to create a sitemap is to visit **http://xml-sitemaps.com** and enter your domain name: their script will crawl your site and create the necessary XML file, and provide reports on any broken links. Once finished, you will have two files: sitemap.xml and sitemap.gz, which is a compressed version of the XML file.

These files need to be uploaded to your webserver's public_html directory, so they are accessible from the URL **http://mysite.com/sitemap.xml** (and .gz). You will need to rebuild the sitemap file every time your content changes, since it only represents a snapshot of your site at the point of crawling.

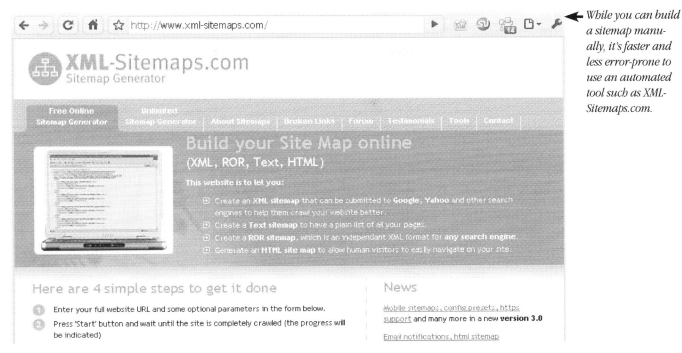

While you can build a sitemap manually, it's faster and less error-prone to use an automated tool such as XML-Sitemaps.com.

Alternatively, many CMS systems have plug-ins which can automate the creation and submission of a sitemap file. In WordPress, the *Google XML Sitemaps* plug-in by Arne Brachhold will generate the XML file every time a page or post is updated and alert Google, Yahoo!, Ask.com and Bing. Even if you are not using a CMS, many web hosting services provide tools that run on a scheduler to achieve the same effect.

To manually submit your sitemap file:

- **Google**: create an account with Google Webmaster Tools (see tip 41) at **http://www.google.com/webmasters/tools** and register your site.

- **Yahoo!**: visit **https://siteexplorer.search.yahoo.com/submit** and click "Submit a Site Feed".

- **Bing**: create an account with Bing Webmaster Center at **http://www.bing.com/webmaster** and register your site.

- **Ask.com**: after your site map is uploaded, go to the following URL: **http://submissions.ask.com/ping?sitemap=http://mysite.com/sitemap.xml** replacing the last part of the URL with your real sitemap location.

ON-PAGE FACTORS

On-page SEO covers the range of factors you have direct control over in the design of your pages and websites. A few years ago, these factors had a considerably greater effect on your position in search engine results pages, but over time have become less of an influence. As these factors became better understood, more and more sites employed them to boost SEO, so Google and other engines have put less emphasis on these over time.

That's not to say that on-page SEO doesn't matter - it does, principally because having good on-page SEO makes your site compare more favorably to those that don't, and at the very least gives you an equal footing with competition employing the same tactics. And there are still a staggering number of sites in the small and medium-sized business arena that don't use on-page SEO to its full effect, so the comparative benefit is worth having.

Here we cover:

- The structure and attribute of each page that will help or hurt search engine rankings.
- Problems associated with duplicate content
- Web server configuration settings.
- Building effective outbound links and using strong anchor text.
- Taking advantage of social sharing buttons on your site.

It's important to understand that on-page SEO is about giving your site the very best opportunity to be evaluated fairly and accurately by the search engine spiders. You are crafting the HTML and structure of your website so that a crawler can assess and navigate all your pages easily and without confusion. Spider algorithms are ultimately just software, and optimizing your pages for that software will ultimately lead to better placement than ignoring how they work.

21 Add a title to your page

The title meta tag the most important on-page element to boost your ranking. The text in the title tells search engines what your page is about.

Possibly one of the easiest of all SEO fixes, yet one of the most commonly overlooked, the title tag is a major determinant of how search engines see your page. The title tag is like the name of a book printed on its cover - no author would have a cover without a title because the book will never get found, yet there are millions of web pages with no title.

The primary reason why the title is important is that search engines put considerable weighting on its content to determine where the page should appear in search results. In some cases the title can be more important than the content on the page to determine its significance. Consequently, the title needs to communicate keywords and relevance for ranking to help ensure the page is indexed properly in the first place.

The second major reason is that a page's title is directly copied into the first line of any search result, so for a visitor to click through the result it needs to be relevant to their search. Search terms that the user has entered in their query will appear **bolded** in the title, so the more terms that match, the more the title will attract their attention.

To optimize the appeal to both search engines and potential visitors, the ideal title tag has the following attributes:

- **Keyword phrases**: unless you have a well known brand, most visitors will search using topical keywords rather than your company name directly. You should ensure that the most likely search terms to find your content appear in the page title.

- **Company name**: your brand should appear in the page title, though you may receive more traffic if it appears after the keyword phrases (eg. "Bay Area Accountant - Beswick Accounting").

- **Brief and descriptive**: don't spam the title with repetitive keyword phrases, and keep the length to around 10-12 words maximum. Search engines prefer shorter titles, and visitors will scan the title for relevance, ignoring unneccesarily long phrases.

- **Unique**: search engines look at pages not sites, so for the best results each page must have a different title, optimized for the keywords on that particular page.

How to modify a web page's title

In an HTML file, the title meta tag is found in the header:

```
<HEAD>
<TITLE>One Uproar - Website design, SEO SEM and Social Media for
your business</TITLE>
</HEAD>
```

In the above example, the title appears in the first line of the search results:

One Uproar - Website Design, **SEO**, SEM and Social Media for your ...
Create a stir online for your business with **One Uproar**. Billions of customers are waiting.
oneuproar.com/ - Cached

Additionally, the title will appear in the title bar of most browsers:

One Uproar - Website Design, SEO, SEM and Social Media for your business - Mozilla Firefox
File   Edit   View   History   Bookmarks   Tools   Help

Web page editing programs will often show the title tag as part of the page properties. The ideal length for a title tag is under 70 characters, though Google will read the whole title tag and truncate longer ones (especially if the search terms are at the end of the title). For best results you should stay under 70 characters, since your goal is to immediately convey what the page is about.

Putting your search keywords towards the beginning of the title tag can sometimes generate more clicks - it's worth testing different titles to see whether company or keywords-first works best. Don't forget you're also writing titles to sell your pages and invite the click, so the title should be appealing to human readers and not just the search engines. You should look at the HTML for *every* page on your site and immediately fix any that have missing or unhelpful titles.

The title tag is also used as the caption for bookmarks. If a user bookmarks your page and it doesn't have a useful reference, chances are they won't return via the bookmark again. This is another good reason to make sure your title is compelling and different for every page.

22 Add a description to your page

The description tag helps visitors as well as search engines understand the content of a page and should be present on every page.

The description tag used to be much more important than it is today and was a major determinant in ranking. Less ethical sites would spam the description with keyword repetition and often provide descriptions that were irrelevant to the page's actual content. Consequently, as search algorithms have become more complex, its usefulness for SEO purposes has declined, and it's not conclusive whether the description influences ranking in Google anymore.

Even so, it's still an important attribute if used properly, since the description is often displayed in search results below the title, acting like a sub-heading to the title. Visitors use the desciption to find out if a page is relevant for their search, so rather than repeating the title, a good description will elaborate on the content. As with the title, it's worth spending the time to craft your copy to motivate people to click.

As with the title, search terms in the query will be automatically bolded; but unlike the title, most search engines will not provide any SEO weight to the description for containing keyword phrases. A good description includes the following attributes:

- **Keyword phrases**: naturally include your most prominent keywords in an unrepetitive way.
- **Brief and descriptive**: provide a succinct sentence that will entice the visitor to explore further, without simply stacking keyword phrases.
- **Unique**: as with the title, a description should apply for one particular page rather than the entire site.

The optimal length of the description is debatable and many seem to agree on 75-125 characters being about right. Personally, I would focus on the appropriate length for a visitort - if you can summarize a page in 50 characters, then why pad it out? Anything considered "too long" by a search engine will be shortened with an elipsis (...), or not used at all and - more importantly.

Although Google doesn't place much significance in the description meta tag anymore, there are some search engines that do. The description gives you a little more screen real estate in the search results, so it pays to take advantage of the extra space to draw visitors to your site.

How to modify a web page's description

In an HTML file, the description meta tag is found in the header:

```
<HEAD>
<META NAME="description" CONTENT="Modern Home Furnishings offers
unique, contemporary, italian, european furniture for your modern
home. Also bedroom, dining & living room sets in Wisconsin, Michi-
gan, Indiana, Iowa areas.</TITLE>
</HEAD>
```

```
4  <title>Unique, Contemporary, Modern, Italian, European Furniture In Chicago, IL</title>
5  <meta name="description" content="Modern Home Furnishings offers unique, contemporary, italian, eu
   bedroom, dining & living room sets in Wisconsin, Michigan, Indiana, Iowa areas.">
6  <meta name="keywords" content="italian furniture in chicago, modern furniture in chicago, contempo
   furniture in chicago, unique furniture in chicago, bedroom, dining sets, living room, Wisconsin, M
7  <meta name="verify-v1" content="ywDppk8sSlosHfKZa1xhGeaCOV/+stPzH4GKuhAH9Vg=" />
8  <meta HTTP-EQUIV="Content-Type" CONTENT="text/html; charset=iso-8859-1">
9  <script language="JavaScript">
```

In this example, the description appears until the title of the search results, and is truncated for length:

Modern Furniture, Contemporary Italian Designer European **Home ...**
Modern furniture, contemporary **furniture**, Italian European **furniture**, designer **furniture**,
home office furnishings & retro **furniture** at online store has ...
Bedroom - Dining Room - Family & Living - Office Furniture
www.spacify.com/ - Cached - Similar

Webpage editing programs will often show the description tag as part of the page properties. There are many instances where Google will disregard your description completely and provide its own version based upon content found on the page, so having a good description is an *attempt* to influence what will be shown rather than any sort of guarantee.

The Keywords meta tag

Whereas both title and description are useful meta tags, *keywords* is no longer used and can be ignored. Google officially doesn't use it anymore (**http://www.mattcutts.com/blog/keywords-meta-tag-in-web-search**), there's no indication that any other major engine does either, and this tag is largely considered defunct in the SEO community. While some people protest its relevance, since it was once a major factor in determining rankings, and it certainly doesn't hurt to include a keywords tag, I wouldn't recommend going to any effort to add it to your web pages.

23 **Using alternative image text**

Visitors can see images but search engines have a better understanding of text - make both happy by describing each image with alternative text.

Images are an essential part of creating good-looking web pages - with the exception of a few sites such as Craigslist.org, most popular sites take advantage of the visual 'pop' provided by graphics. But although images are essential for visitor-friendly design, search engines cannot look at a picture and determine its content or relevance.

From an SEO perspective, you should always use text wherever possible since it's spider-friendly, but where there are key images, you should use the ALT tag to describe what they are. Even for images that appear to be text, such as company logos or graphical headlines, spiders will only understand the content with some assistance. For e-commerce sites with pictures of products for sale, this tip is especially important in order to associate the images with the item's name and description.

The ALT tag and image file name

Image recognition is a long way behind the semantic analysis of text, and so many images are untagged that it's not hard to push images onto the first page of image results.

Entering the phrase "Antique lamp" into Google, the first image result is on **http://www.theantiquesite.net/antique-lighting** (right) and the image is properly tagged with the ALT text "Antique lamp" (below). Additionally, the image has the file name "antique-lamp-btm.jpg", reinforcing the phrase "antique lamp".

View the page source to see the underlying HTML and ALT tags.

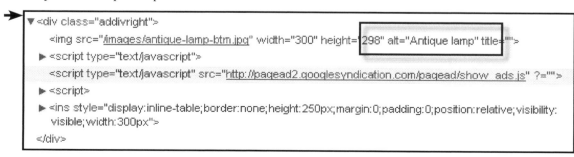

ALT text is another controversial SEO element that many say doesn't matter anymore, but Google has confirmed that the ALT text and filename is used.

Despite how many images appear on web pages, relatively few use the ALT tag. In addition to helping SEO, alternative text is also displayed when the visitor hovers over the image with the mouse, and or if the browser has images disabled. Many users in bandwidth-constrained situations (or on some cell phones) either have images switched off or they will see the alternative text before the full image loads. In many HTML editors, the ALT property is available as a right-click option or property sheet for an image. In direct HTML, the alternative text tag part of the IMG element:

```
<IMG SRC="carpet.png" ALT="Persian Rug">
```

In terms of how you should describe an image in ALT text:

- Think about what you would like to have displayed if images weren't available: "My Company's Logo" isn't as useful as "John Dough's Pizza".

- Make the description useful for the image standing alone outside of the site since it will appear in image results without any supporting information.

- If the graphic is purely decorative, such as spacer graphics or bullet images, say nothing. It doesn't add meaning to describe a 50-pixel illustrative red line.

- Keep the description keyword-focused and succinct: "Signature Cappuccino" is more effective than "one of our famous custom-made specialty espresso beverages".

Definitely take advantage of the ability to give meaning to graphics but don't abuse it - just because search engines can't decipher images doesn't mean they're not sophisticated:

- Don't be tempted to use unhelpful keyword-stuffed descriptions that a human would immediately see as spam.

- Don't create blank, empty or invisible images (1 pixel by 1 pixel) and give these keyword-rich descriptions, which is a form of cloaking.

Your site will get penalized if you get caught - and if you don't get caught today, you'll get caught at some point in the future as the algorithms change. Image recognition is getting more sophisticated, so use the ALT tag to reinforce your keywords in a positive way.

Watch Google's Matt Cutts explain how Google uses ALT text at http://www. mattcutts.com/blog/matt-video-alt-attributes-for-images/

24 Embed quality outbound links

Google, especially, is all about links. Help GoogleBot understand what your content is about by reinforcing your copy with relevant links to other sites.

Increasingly, sites are obsessing with inbound links. I receive upwards of a dozen emails a day asking me to exchange links with other sites with the idea that we each point to each other in symbiotic link-ship. There's no problem with relevant link exchanges: if you are a hotel and the local visitors' center wants to trade links, this is a win-win from an SEO perspective, since clearly the sites and content are related. Conversely, trading links with unrelated sites just for the sake of liking does not help - a hotel in Florida pointing to a lighting shop in Oregon has zero value and could potentially hurt SEO.

Understand then that outbound links are about reinforcing your keywords and content. Our hotel in Florida will want to appear on a page in the Visitor Center's website that is about hotels in Florida. This kind of linkage is one of the strongest, most effective ways to build credibility and ranking with Google - which makes complete sense, since users would view the relationship between these sites as useful, complimentary and relevant.

Outbound links do not have to be reciprical to be worthwhile - if your video store has a blog discussing a new movie called *SEO Crime Squad*, then linking to the title in IMDB is a great idea. There are two ways to create these links, one of which is much more effective than the other:

- The Bad Way: "Rent out SEO Crime Squad and read exclusive interviews from the movie here".
- The Good Way: "Read IMDB's Exclusive Interview from SEO Crime Squad and rent it out today."

The difference between the two types of anchor text (the underlined text that represents the link) is that, in the first, the keyword 'here' doesn't mean anything in terms of describing the link. In the second, the phrase is the title of the IMDB article, it's keyword-rich and explains the connection. Since you control the anchor-text, it also reinforces the topic of the third-party page.

Regardless of your page topic, you can 'train' Google to understand the context of your content better by linking to relevant pages that reinforce your topic's relevance. Like everything in SEO, overdoing is sometimes worse than not doing it at all, but a handful of good links will help your rankings.

Using 'nofollow'

Search engines are based around links and will follow links on your pages to discover their contents and build a semantic connection between the two. Ideally, your selection of outbound links includes quality, relevant sources so your web page becomes a place of authority for a given subject. When the content of your pages is under your control, you generally wouldn't be concerned about dubious links becoming part of your site. The *nofollow* attribute is used to tell a search engine whether to follow a link on your page: for untrusted links, you should use nofollow.

This is fine when your site about Maltese puppies has links to the Humane Society and SPCA, but more of a problem if your site has a forum, allows comments, reviews or other user-generated content. In this case, users can create links in their contributions that may direct your pages to spam, porn or phishing sites - and being associated with those sites doesn't help your SEO ranking. While you can moderate user content and remove spam, it's often easier to use nofollow to disassociate yourself with links posted by users.

The nofollow attribute essentially tells a search engine to ignore the link and not to follow the reference. Search engines may well have a more sophisticated approach to decide if the nofollow is relevant, and choose to follow the link anyway in certain cases, but it pays to indicate if your site endorses links that may or may not be appropriate.

The simplest way to look at this is:

- Don't use the 'no-follow' attribute for trusted links that are part of your web page. Trying to use this attribute to show Google which pages are important is largely unnecessary (for example, nofollowing a link to your privacy policy is not needed).

- Do use it for untrusted links, such as those provided by visitors, that can be subject to spammers and bots trying to take advantage of your link. Most visitors will be unaware that their links are defaulted to nofollow so if the occasional "bad link" slips through, at least your site is indicating it doesn't want to be associated.

Setting this up isn't nearly as technical as it sounds - the nofollow attribute looks like this in HTML:

```
<a href="http://www.dubious.com/" rel="nofollow">cheap pills</a>.
```

If your pages are becoming targeted by spammers in comments, reviews or forums, it is probably worth investigating other mechanisms for blocking their contributions in the first place - such as CAPTCHA or human moderation.

(H1) 25 Headers and semantic formatting

(H2) Headers tags and semantic text formatting provide another subtle way to indicate topical relevance.

(H3) What's a Header Tag?

Header tags are used by search engines to understand the structure and topical content of a given page. Header tags have a hierarchical level of importance with H1 being the top-level and H6 being the lowest - you are unlikely to use all six headers in one page, but usage of H1 and H2 is common. If this page were a web page, you can see in the left margin which text would wrapped in header tags.

While most pages have titles, there's a subtle difference between a what visually appears as a title and what is defined as a header tag. For example, consider the three apparently identical headings below:

If books had header tags, on this page the tip title would be H1, subtitle H2 and paragraph headers H3.

- The first is an H1 header:

  ```
  <h1>My Company</h1>
  ```

- The second is a regular paragraph formatted with inline CSS and HTML to make the text larger and bold:

  ```
  <p style="font-family: Arial, Helvetica,
  sans-serif; font-size: x-large"><strong>My
  Company</strong></p>
  ```

- The third is an image:

  ```
  <p><img src="MyCompany.png" width="155" height="34"/></p>
  ```

My Company

My Company

My Company

For SEO, the first version is the best option, indicating an H1 header in the HTML. The second ranks in the middle, since at least it uses some semantic formatting to indicate significance. Meanwhile the image - one of the most common ways companies show titles - has no significance at all, since spiders can't read images and the HTML doesn't indicate anything of importance. So even though all three would appear the same to a visitor, each is dramatically different for SEO.

Incidentally, header tags don't have to be ugly! You can use CSS to make H1-H6 tags attractive. Although you won't find adding header tags will dramatically change your rankings, using them has become a standard practice, and I'd strongly advise checking all your pages to ensure you have at the very least a top-level H1 tag.

Semantic formatting

If you've ever used with HTML, you'll likely know that:

```
<B>Hello</B>
<I>Goodbye</I>
```

...appears as **Hello** followed by *Goodbye*. This markup basically tells the browser how to format what appears in between the tags, but doesn't indicate to a search engine spider that what is being marked up has any significance in terms of meaning.

There are two more tags that visually have the same result but search engines interpret slightly differently, namely:

```
<STRONG>I'm Bolded</STRONG>
<EM>I'm Italicized</EM>
```

These also would appear as **I'm Bolded** followed by *I'm Italicized*.

The difference is subtle and doesn't equate to simply replacing <B> with <STRONG> and <I> with <EM> throughout your site. Where there are significant keyword phrases, it pays to use these semantic tags, but not where you are only intending to make formatting differences.

For example, if you have a field that reads **Your Name Here**, visually it may make sense to differentiate its appearance with bold text, but the phrase is probably not connected with your SEO effort, so doesn't deserve the semantic emphasis.

If this seems complicated or difficult to implement in your site, don't sweat it - emphasis and strong emphasis are not major elements in the way search engines view your pages. But like so many techniques they offer a minor way to influence how spiders determine the meaning of your content. Search engine spiders want to know the meaning of your website, so help them understand when the semantic emphasis matches the visual emphasis a human reader would see.

Both headers and semantic formatting are beneficial for SEO, but more importantly they improve the user's experience of your site by segmenting content logically and emphasizing key words and phrases.

For more information, visit http://searchengineland.com/overlooked-but-beneficial-on-page-seo-elements-38286.

26 Check your page width and height

Visitors have different screen resolutions, so designing for the most common sizes will give the majority the best viewing experience.

If you've noticed text getting smaller and smaller on your computer screen over the years, this is due to screen resolutions getting higher. The resolution determines how many pixels appear on the monitor, and the higher the number, the more can be crammed onto the display. Put simply, if you design your pages for a higher resolution than the majority of your audience uses, they will have to scroll to see the whole content of the page.

As of January 2010, w3schools.com reports that 96% of web users have a display that's 1024 pixels (width) by 768 (height) or better (**http://www.w3schools.com/browsers/browsers_display.asp**). Consequently, it makes sense to optimize your design for 1024x768 since this balances the ability to display more content with appearance for the largest number of your visitors. For data specifically about *your* visitors, you can see this information in Google Analytics (see tip 42 about setting this up on your site).

Google Analytics collects browser statistics from your site's visitors.

Google's Browser Size Tool

To see what percentage of Internet users can view your webpages without scrolling, visit **http://browsersize.googlelabs.com** and enter your domain name (or a page URL). The web page will be overlaid with a grid showing screen width and height, and the cumulative percentage of users who can view that size.

Specifically, the sizes shown here don't represent the entire screen resolution, but the browser size less space for toolbars, window titles and so forth. Since many users don't maximize their browser window, the optimal width and height reported may be considerably smaller in this tool than you might expect.

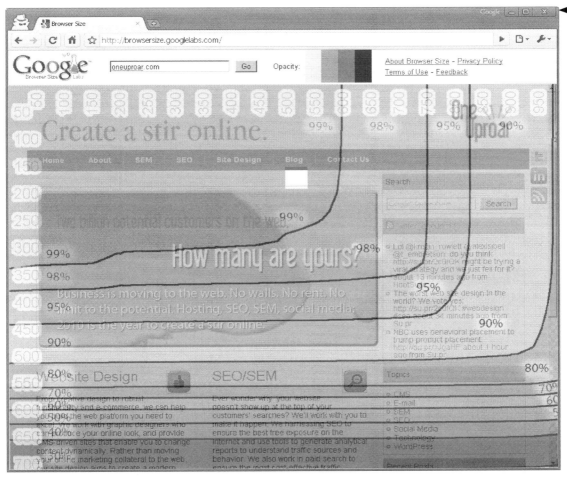

◄— This webpage is 960 pixels wide, so it's optimized to fit in a 1024-pixel wide screen resolution, but only 90% of visitors can see its width.

One solution to the width problem is use a *liquid layout*, which adjusts the layout of the page depending on how wide the client browser is stretched. This is managed by representing the layout in percentages rather than pixel-specified sizes, so page elements are positioned dynamically when the page is rendered by the browser. These layouts can be harder to design initially but solve the width problem quite elegantly.

For examples and resources on liquid layouts, visit http://www.cssliquid.com.

Page height

Height is another concern - vertical content that can only be viewed by scrolling will receive less attention than the part of the page 'above the fold'. While web pages tend to be taller than the browser window, it's essential that the important parts of your page, such as navigation, shopping cart management and "Pay Now" buttons, be placed as close to the top of the page as possible to receive the maximum number of clicks.

Google Analytics has a useful site overlay tool that shows which links on a page your visitors are clicking. Integrating the data collected about your site's usage, the tool allows you to see immediately what the most popular links are.

The Google Analytics click overlay shows which links visitors are clicking. The links nearer the top tend to receive the most clicks.

What are visitors looking at?

There are some interesting eye-tracking studies observing how web surfers look at a browser page. Given the sheer information overload we are all faced with, our surfing style has evolved to extract the maximum information out of a page in the smallest amount of time. This creates a disconnect between designers and visitors, since pages are usually built to look aesthetically pleasing but are not optimized for the reading style of the average visitor.

It's debatable how useful eye-tracking studies are but much of data I've seen from Google Analytics supports their design conclusions. One of the key observations in these studies is that users read across the page in a 'F' shape, scanning the top first, moving down the left, scanning the middle, and then down the left to the bottom. There is considerably more attention paid to the top left of the page and top in general than anywhere else, while the bottom right is largely ignored.

Based upon this, when you design your web pages, you should keep in mind:

- The first paragraph of text is the one most likely to be read, so put your important information here. As you progress down through the copy, less and less will be read. This is also consistent with one theory about Google's keyword analysis, which shows words at the top of the page have more weighting in the algorithm that those further down.

- When visitors **scan text**, bolded phrases **catch their attention**, so make sure to use bold text as a guide to **what to expect**. These bold snippets can tell the broad story of your copy without having to read the whole thing.

- Users rapidly skip through headings as a guide to content, so following the advice in tip 25 helps locate the information needed more quickly. Be sure to break up your copy in small chunks with plenty of headings as a guide (more than you would naturally use in printed material).

- People read bullet points and lists, possibly one of the reasons that "Top 10" lists have become so popular in searches. Where possible, break the information into concise bullets (3-5 points ideally), or numbered lists of items.

- Graphics are generally ignored as users have become trained to ignore banners and other advertisements, but they are drawn to close-up pictures of faces. If the top of your web page is a banner ad, you are missing a major opportunity to use the screen real estate more effectively.

- Text is viewed more than graphics: the 80/20 rule suggests that 80% of a web page should be text, with only 20% graphics. If you find your design becoming graphic-heavy, this isn't good for retaining the visitor's attention (or for SEO, which is largely text-driven).

27 **Build a good .htaccess file**

Available on most web servers, .htaccess is a powerful file that can solve a range of technical SEO issues.

The .htaccess file provides configuration information for the web server and can help address a wide variety of issues from security to URL redirection that have an impact on SEO. Generally, if your server runs on Unix or Linux or any version of the Apache web server, you can use .htaccess (incidentally, Windows servers have their own methods of handling most of the issues raised here).

Its capabilities are well documented, and it's a human-readable text file that's easily to modify through any notepad-type application. Use an FTP client such as FileZilla (**http://filezilla-project.org**) to download your .htaccess and make changes (ensure you first make a backup in case you need to revert back to the original copy).

Rewriting URLs

In tip 5, I mentioned that human-friendly URLs are also SEO friendly, so http://mysite.com/products-shoes.htm is preferable to http://mysite.com/products.php?product_type=shoes. The latter version contains a parameter used by the site to determine the product type selected by the user, but it can be written to look like the first URL using .htaccess directives. The ability to rewrite URLs is very powerful and very complicated. Since it makes extensive use of *regular expressions*, you should seek technical help before making any changes on your production (live) website.

301 Redirects

If you move pages on your site from one location to another, it can seriously affect your website rankings when the search engines find the content is missing. While it's possible to update the links on your own site, as the number of inbound links grows it's virtually impossible to have these all updated to reflect the new location.

The easiest way to handle this is with a 301 redirect, which is the technical equivalent of a change of address form at the post office. URLs that have moved will automatically be redirected to the new location of the file without needing to notify the referring sites. Although there are other ways to redirect traffic, this is definitely the most SEO-friendly way and arguably the easiest to implement.

The syntax is quite simple and only requires one line to redirect one URL:

```
redirect 301 /old/mypage.htm http://mysite.com/new/mypage.htm
```

This instructs the web server to point any traffic from the first URL to the second URL. If your URL contains spaces, simply enclose the URL in quotes like this:

```
redirect 301 "/old/my page.htm" http://mysite.com/new/mypage.htm
```

In the event that your entire site is moved from one domain to another, you don't need to create 301 redirects for each page or resource on the server - the following line will redirect all traffic from one domain to a new domain:

```
redirect 301 / http://www.mysite.com/
```

In this case, the redirect preserves the directories and filenames so that a visitor to http://oldsite.com/pages/contact.htm would arrive at http://www.mysite.com/pages/contact.htm.

Solving the canonical naming problem

Duplicate content is a major problem (see tip 28), and one of the main sources is that http://mysite.com and http://www.mysite.com both point to exactly the same web page. It's a good idea to decide before building a website whether you prefer the www or non-www version of the domain name (personally, I prefer non-www but many users still believe the www is necessary).

The following code will redirect all non-www traffic to the www version:

```
RewriteEngine on

RewriteCond %{HTTP_HOST} ^mysite.com [NC]

RewriteRule ^(.*)$ http://www.mysite.com/$1 [R=301,L]
```

Redirecting traffic based upon language

If you have sites in several languages, it's easy to redirect the visitor to the version in their language, based upon information sent by their browser in the "Accept-Language" variable. For example, to redirect traffic to http://mysite.com to http://mysite.fr for French users, add the following:

```
RewriteEngine on

RewriteCond %{HTTP:Accept-Language} (fr) [NC]

RewriteRule .* http://mysite.fr [R,L]
```

This is based on browser language - not geography - so will only work if the language has been set.

Blocking Bad Bots

There are many programs on the Internet that crawl websites for a variety of reasons, and some of the more malicious will attempt to harvest your site's content for reproduction on spam-oriented sites. Apart from the duplicate content issue and copyright violations, these crawlers are using your server's resources for no good reason.

You can block these bad bots by adding the following lines to the .htaccess file:

```
RewriteEngine on

RewriteCond %{HTTP_REFERER} ^http(s)?://(www\.)?mysite.com.*$ [NC]

RewriteRule .* - [F,L]
```

Preventing image theft

Image theft occurs when a third-party site links to one of your graphics in their web page - although the image appears in their web page and their visitors are unaware that it's provided by a your site, it's a drain on your website's bandwidth and processing power with no benefit to you.

This is known as hotlinking and, from an SEO standpoint, it's bad because it can slow down your site (or even make it completely unavailable in extreme cases). To block offending sites from embedding your images without your permission, add the following to the .htaccess file:

```
RewriteEngine on

RewriteCond %{HTTP_REFERER} !^$

RewriteCond %{HTTP_REFERER} !^http(s)?://(www\.)?yourdomain.com
[NC]

RewriteRule \.(jpg|jpeg|png|gif)$ -
[NC,F,L]
```

You can optionally display an alternate image (perhaps a message indicating that the site is trying to hotlink, such as the one shown on the right) by changing the last line above to this (replace the bolded text with the actual image URL):

```
RewriteRule \.(jpg|jpeg|png|gif)$ http://
mysite.com/dont-steal.gif [NC,R,L]
```

This person was hot-linking this image & stealing bandwidth.

Hotlinking cost us $300 extra a month. Could you afford paying for everyone wanting to hotlink to your files?

Handle common webserver errors elegantly to keep visitors on your site.

Custom error pages

A variety of errors can occur when your web server attempts to handle a request - some of the most common include:

- **404**: the resource in the URL wasn't found (the technical version of "Not here").
- **403**: the client is forbidden from accessing the URL for some reason.
- **400:** bad request.
- **500**: an unexpected error occurred.
- **401**: accessing the requested page requires user authentication first.

It's a good idea to handle these errors graciously by diverting the visitor to a specific error-handling page that includes the site's regular navigation and searching options, so they can try again without leaving your site. To show your custom error page, add the following line to your .htaccess file:

```
ErrorDocument 404 http://mysite.com/404.html
```

This example shows the web page at http://mysite.com/404.html whenever a 404 error occurs, and you need to change the error number and URL for each error you want to handle.

For documentation on .htaccess syntax, visit http://httpd.apache.org/docs/ trunk/howto/htaccess.html. To generate .htaccess content automatically, use the tools available at http://www.htaccesstools.com.

28 **Avoid duplicate content**

Search engines detect duplicate content and delist the copied pages, so make sure your content is unique.

Search engines try to provide diversity in their results so they omit results that are broadly the same. They realize that user don't want the results page spammed with identical entries, nor do they want to waste resources on crawling content that exists elsewhere. The other reason while content duplication is policed aggressively by search engines is that many spam sites use duplication to funnel more traffic to the same page, so that several hundred identical sites are set up with different domain names to optimize for keyword variants.

Duplicate content is detected when the same material is available via multiple URLs, and there's no guarantee which URL will be indexed and which will be ignored. Incidentally, the content doesn't have to be identical to be considered a duplicate - search engines have algorithms that measure the similarity of two sets of data, so copying a reasonable quantity of information from one page to another may be considered a duplication. The same is true for common resources, such as images, PDFs and video, which are covered in Google's 2006 patent on detecting duplication.

Using manufacturers' product descriptions

When multiple e-commerce sites sell the same products, it's common to use the boilerplate descriptions provided by the product's manufacturer. Mixed with common additional information, such as ISBNs, model numbers, authors names and supporting links, this can make the product page on one site look substantially similar to the others. This is true even if the containing page looks very different in terms of layout and graphics. If your product pages aren't ranking when competitors selling the same product are appearing in the results, you need to invest the time to rewrite the descriptions.

Print-only versions of the page

Many sites offer print-optimized versions of their web pages, so the printed output is formatted more neatly than the browser-only version. The side-effect of this practice is that two URLs point to almost exactly the same page, so search engines will flag this as duplication. The easiest way to manage this problem is to modify your robots.txt file (see tip 41) to exclude the print-only URLs from the crawlers. If the duplicate page is already being indexed, you should use the meta "noindex" tag in the HTML header to indicate to request its removal from returning crawlers.

Mirror sites

For sites serving larger numbers of users, one load-balancing technique involves using mirror sites, which are essentially site duplicates copied across on different servers. Clearly, this is a case of duplication intended to help users but search engines are very likely to ignore the mirrors in their search results. Although there are many good reasons to use mirror sites, these days there are good alternative methods available in most cases (which are technically beyond the scope of this book).

For more on mirror sites, see Wikipedia's article at http://en.wikipedia.org/wiki/ Mirror_(computing).

Multiple URLs

The biggest cause of unintentional duplication is the fact that most pages on most sites can be reached by multiple URLs. For example, these URLs all point to the same page:

- http://mysite.com
- http://mysite.com/index.htm
- https://mysite.com
- https://mysite.com/index.htm

If inbound (or internal) links point to more than one of these variants, the duplicate content flag will be raised. Unethical competitors can even use this flaw against you by adding the variants as inbound links from other sites, causing a detrimental effect to your site's SEO. To avoid this problem, create a sitemap file (see tip 20) and ensure you have a good .htaccess file in place (see tip 27).

Another variant on this is the canonical domain name problem, meaning that http://www.mysite.com and http://mysite.com (without the www) resolve to the same page. This is actually a huge problem that's relatively easy to address, since you can use the .htaccess file to set a preference so that the URL will be rewritten to the preferred version. Additionally, you can inform Google through Google Webmaster Tools (see tip 41) on which version to use. Ideally, these steps should be in place before your site goes live, since it's considerably hard to track down and redirect multiples URLs after they have become linked and indexed.

If you are using WordPress, install the Permanent Redirect Plug-in available at http://scott.yang.id.au/code/permalink-redirect/.

Inclusion of content through server-side scripting

This is less common but worth mentioning. If a page uses server side script to include other feeds, such as RSS, crawlers will see the feed content as it's created by the server as part of the response. The problem is that the feed is showing content that has been published elsewhere, so appears to be a duplication to the search engine.

A simple solution is to retrieve the feed uses client-side code since spiders don't execute code on page they crawl, so the feed would appear to a human visitor but not a crawler. Incidentally, this is one of the few legitimate uses of showing one type of content to a spider and another to a visitor.

Session IDs and variables in URLs

Some of techniques used by websites to track state and database parameters, such as session IDs and variables in GET posts, are problematic in creating the impression of multiple URLs leading to the same content. For example:

- http://mysite.com/page.html?session=12 and http://mysite.com/page.html?session=13 represent two different sessions for the same page, but are seen as two distinct URLs.

- http://mysite.com/page.html?Cat=1&Product=2 can be rewritten by switching variables around as http://mysite.com/page.html?Product=2&Cat=1, which makes no difference to the web site but again appears as two URLs to search engines.

For this reason, it's important to make sure that search bots can navigate your site without session IDs or tracking variables to prevent errant duplication problems.

Too much commonality across web pages

Many sites use templates to ensure all web pages have a common look, and may repeat headers, logos, company information, testimonials and so forth on every page. This is especially true for e-commerce sites, where 100 products are shown in 100 pages but the bulk of each page is the same, so it appears that there are 100 duplicates.

Although templates help with consistency and the user's experience, it's important to ensure that each page has its own distinction meta title (see tip 21) and meta description (see tip 22), and that enough content changes between each page to be considered distinct. How much is 'enough' is open to debate, but if only the product's titles changes and every other element is part of a template, it's very likely a spider won't see any value in indexing most of the site.

Syndication

Many sites syndicate their blogs and white papers to reach a broader audience and drive traffic back to the original site. Since the articles are often repeated verbatim, the danger is that these may be seen as duplicate URLs. This wouldn't necessarily matter if the original site's URL remained listed and the syndicated sites didn't, but there's no guarantee that the reverse will happen and the original URL becomes flagged as a copy.

Copyright infringement

Believe it or not, there are programs running on the Internet that crawl web pages just like a search engine spider with the express intention of use the content to fill spam sites. Apart from being annoying, the duplication can be very harmful to your SEO efforts, since potentially your pages may get delisted as duplicates while the spam site stays in the index.

To protect images, you can make a modification to the .htaccess file that goes a long way to prevent image theft and *hotlinking* (linking to your image from another site, but using your bandwidth and CPU time) - see tip 27 for more details.

For other content, services such as **http://copyscape.com** offer a simple way to check if your material has been stolen. Copyscape can help find these sites, and their premium services offer effective methods to constantly police your copyrighted content, and send take-down notices if needed.

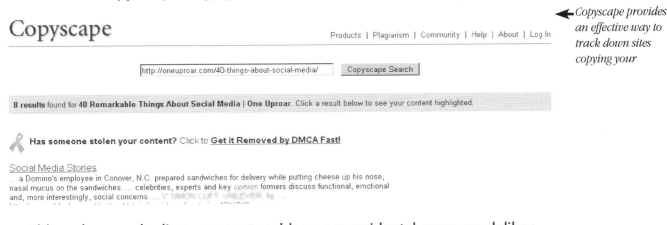

Copyscape provides an effective way to track down sites copying your

Although many duplicate content problems are accidental, some are deliberate in attempt to boost rankings. Put simply, as Google Webmaster Guidelines states: "Don't create multiple pages, subdomains, or domains with substantially duplicate content."

29 Use keywords in anchor text

While links provide the semantic structure of the Internet, the description of a link provides context.

Spiders crawl pages and follow the links discovered on those pages - this technique enables them to build a structure of pages and how they relate to each other, separately from how those pages are structured on their own sites. The interlinking of pages forms the semantic structure of the web and is largely responsible for how search engines determine the relevance and value of their results.

You are probably used to seeing links on a page as blue underlined sections of text, and this formatting difference is intended to indicate to the visitor that there's a link to follow. When you examine the HTML that forms the link "Want to know more about our product? Click here!", it looks like this:

```
Want to know more about our product? Click <a href="http://mysite.
com/product.html">here</a>!
```

The word "here" in this example is called anchor text, and it's one of the most significant indicators used by search engines to consider relevance. Consequently, using "here" or "click here" for anchor text is a wasted opportunity to influence search engine rankings, yet it's one of the most common ways to provide a link. A much better way to link to your pages is use your keywords in your anchor text - for example, "ABC's Document Storage Services has excellent pricing."

At its simplest, having many pages pointing to your web page with the same (or similar) keywords reinforces the association between those keywords and your page. Although you don't have much control over the anchor text used by third-parties referencing your web page, you should ensure that all anchor text under your control reinforces the keywords chosen for your site:

- **Internal links**: make sure that links on your pages that point to other pages on your site have good anchor text (e.g. for a law firm, "Legal Services" is better than "Services"). Double-check that there are no "click here" links, since these tend to creep in as content changes.

- **Requested links**: where you have requested a link from a third party, provide the exact HTML you would like to see on their page. Apart from the fact it's easier to cut-and-paste the link than build from scratch, you can provide the precise anchor text you would like to see.

- **Site navigation**: although menu names must be descriptive, a link referring to your site's homepage as "Home" only reinforces a connection between your web page and "Home" rather than the keywords specific to that page.

- **Badges, widgets and icons**: if your site provides any sort of media for third parties, such as widgets, affiliate banners or images, provide the entire HTML complete with anchor text.
- **Review sites, Wikipedia and directories**: if you are providing the listing or description for your business or topic in a directory or review site, ensure your entry uses anchor text appropriately. The same is true for Wikipedia, though most website owners wouldn't qualify for a Wikipedia entry.

While there is some debate within the SEO community over how important anchor text can be, there's a very strong case for taking advantage of its prominence. Anchor text is the number one ranking factor in a 2009 SEOmoz.org survey of SEO consultants (**http://www.seomoz.org/article/search-ranking-factors**).

Additionally, for very competitive keyword phrases, anchor text seems to be the deciding factor in which page receives the higher ranking, especially if the inbound link comes from pages with good PageRank or ranking on its own keyword terms. The more you can associate links with your chosen keyword phrases and topic, the better your SEO for those linked pages.

Google Bombs

Anchor text is so important in search engine rankings, that it's responsible for the highly-publicized *Google bombs* which used the technique to associate given phrases with particular web pages. In a Google bomb, there's a concerted effort to create hundreds of links to a page with misleading anchor text, so searching on the anchor text causes the page to rank first in the search engines. The net effect is that pages can erroneously appear for search terms that aren't related.

The most famous example linked the keyword phrase "miserable failure" with George W Bush's presidential biography. Even though the phrase obviously appeared nowhere on the target website, there were so many inbound links using it as anchor text that it ranked number one. The White House moved the page to a general section about the currently seated President, and for a short while President Obama's page appeared with the same term.

Google has taken steps over the years to combat Google bombing tactics, so the results for "miserable failure" have been corrected. Still, there are many smaller Google bombs still working out there and one SEO expert has cornered the phrase "coolest guy" to prove the point. Anchor text remains extremely important and it's still possible to rank for phrases that don't even appear on a web page.

One company called Click Here has taken advantage of the tendency for unhelpful anchor text: search for "Click Here" on Google and see their ranking.

30 Add social sharing buttons

Visitors boost your SEO by sharing your web page with others - help them do this with sharing buttons.

With the growth of social networks, the way visitors share links and content with each other has changed. When the Internet first became popular, emailing hyperlinks was the primary way to send pages to friends and colleagues. Although this still happens, visitors are increasingly using Facebook, Twitter, Reddit, StumbleUpon and others services to spread web pages they like. One study shows that shared links now account for as much as 33% of traffic driven by search.

Sharing has two important influences on how visitors react to your content:

- **Trust**: in situations where there's a friendship tree or relationship between the sharer and recipient, the recipient is significantly more likely to follow and trust the link because it came from somebody they know. Unlike traffic from search engine queries, the time spent viewing a page and the number of pages views is significantly highly in share referrals. For e-commerce sites, visitors are significantly more like to buy products based upon social recommendations.

- **Reach**: where sharers and recipients don't know each other and "recommended sites" are based upon aggregation of recommendations (such as Digg, Reddit and StumbleUpon), each action of sharing is like a vote. Web pages with the most votes receive substantial third-party traffic, even though the visitors don't know all the people who shared your link. This enables web sites to reach a large audience that's otherwise unlikely to find their content.

Social sharing can produce such increases in traffic that many websites have crashed due to suddenly appearing on the front page of Digg. To take advantage on the growth and impact of sharing, your web pages should make it as easy as possible for visitors to share content they like, so adding social buttons and icons helps a visitor do this with a single click. There are several ways to add the buttons:

- **Manual HTML coding**: website developers can add the icons and submission buttons directly onto your site, as shown on the right by One Uproar's social media links. These have been written into the template and appear in the same place on every page site-wide.

- **Plug-ins**: if you're using a CMS, most now have plug-ins that automate the inclusion of social sharing buttons. TweetMeme is one example (shown top-right), which dynamically counts the number of times an article or pages has been Tweeted, and clicking the icon allows the visitor to instantly Tweet the page to followers.

Twitter Updates

- **Widgets and pre-built HTML**: AddToAny.com and ShareThis.com both provide interfaces to build a share button which includes most social sharing services. The button is fully customizable and you simply paste the resulting HTML into the web page template.

AddToAny and ShareThis both offer the benefit of providing one central location to share seamlessly, replacing the need to code a range of icons and links for different services. As shown above, the icon expands when the visitor hovers over it, saving screen real estate and automatically including new networks and services as they become available.

For more on the influence of social search, see Brian Solis' excellent article at http://www.briansolis.com/2010/03/optimizing-brands-for-social-search/

OFF-PAGE FACTORS

On-page SEO represents the range of factors you have direct control over in designing your web pages and sites. Conversely, 'off-page' elements are everything outside your website relating to your domain, and have become significantly more important for SEO in recent years.

A successful SEO strategy must address off-page elements , so here we cover:

- Techniques for finding quality inbound links to your site, and increasing your site's PageRank by associating with authoritative web pages.

- Using press releases to attract media interest and additional visitors beyond regular search engine traffic.

- Building profiles in social networking sites such as Facebook, LinkedIn and Twitter, and using these networks to engage and interact with existing and potential customers.

- Creating a presence in Google Local Business, and using their analytics to learn more about how visitors find your business.

- Using online directories, submitting listings and generating additional inbound links with high PageRank scores.

Off-page SEO requires more effort than managing on-page factors, but ultimately can help maintain a page-one SERPs ranking, and bring new traffic to your site.

31 Find quality backlinks to your site.

Quality inbound links provide the "link juice" to get traffic. Cultivating links is the backbone of SEO.

Hyperlinks provide the structure of the Internet. For visitors, the vast majority of pages and sites are discovered through hyperlinks from other sites, and for search engines, most content is found by crawling links and indexing new pages that are found. There are two types of links relevant to SEO:

- **Outbound links**, which are the ones on your site leading to external pages, are an important part of the link building process - you should include quality, relevant outbound links throughout your site.

- **Inbound links**, also known as backlinks, which are a more significant contributor to SEO since search engines consider them a signal to relevance. Inbound links are hosted by other websites pointing to yours, which makes them harder to create and control.

Additionally, there are two major reasons why backlinks matter so much to SEO:

- **Semantic relevance**: sites discussing the same or similar topics to yours provide a "thumbs-up" or a vote by linking to your site. Logically, the more votes you have, the more relevance your page has around the given topic.

- **PageRank (PR)**, which is a signal of authority exclusive to Google, is shared with outbound links. If a site with a high PR links to your's, some of that authority is inherited by association.

PageRank is authority, not SEO

There's confusion and bad information in the SEO world relating to PageRank (PR), and there are services peddling PR as the solution to all SEO, which it definitely isn't. A PR score for any given page is a rating between 0 and 10 and although it's calculated continuously in Google's algorithm is only published to the world periodically. Since PR is calculated for every page in the index, very few pages on the web rank above 4 or 5, so it's not uncommon to see low numbers for most pages.

The major reason to be concerned about PageRank is that high-scoring pages linking to you helps build credibility. The theory goes that an authoritative page, measured in PR, would only link to similarly high-quality pages, so those links are most trusted and valuable that links from low PR pages. So when finding pages that are good candidates for linking to yours, it doesn't hurt to consider their PR score. Fundamentally, this is the only way of increasing your own PageRank.

Most importantly, just a couple of high PR pages linking to your site will have a significantly higher impact on your authority and relevance that thousands of low PR, low quality links (which may be considered spam). Finding these candidate links should be a high priority in your SEO work.

First, to determine the PR of a page, install Google's toolbar in the FireFox browser (visit **http://toolbar.google.com** for instructions). Once installed, visit the page in question and wait for the green PR icon to show in the toolbar. When you hover over this, the PR value is displayed (see below). There are other tools that can capture PR, but the Google Toolbar is the only official source.

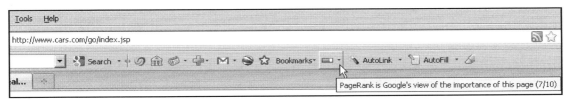

Potential sources for quality backlinks

One of the most important jobs in SEO is to maximize the number of high quality, relevant backlinks to help your page gain authority on a subject. I repeat this mainly to warn you against purchasing thousands of links from services purporting to help your site's SEO, or participating in link farms, link exchanges or other sites that artificially attempt to boost your relevance.

Depending upon your industry, there are many sources for good backlinks:

- Trade associations, chambers of commerce, local business groups.

- City guides, tourism sites and business directories.

- Newspapers, magazines, journals, online encyclopedias, influential bloggers, forums and article directories.

- Vendors and customers.

- Social media sites, social bookmarking and user reviews pages.

- Competitor sites (see who is linking to your competitors).

Once you have identified potential link sources, approach each site administrator with an email requesting a link, and craft the email so it appears personal rather than a bulk message sent to thousands of sites. In most cases, you should provide the incentive of offering a reciprocal link back, since there's no reason why quality sources should not point to each other, and you should also include your name and contact details.

When requesting the link state the entire HTML, such as:

```
<p>Learn the secrets to <a href="http://mywebsite.com/pet-insur-
ance.html">saving money on pet insurance</a>.</p>
```

This helps make the addition of the link as simple as possible for the site's administrator, and also gives you control over the anchor text used (see tip 29).

In other cases, especially in social media, adding a link can be as simple as creating a profile for your site and asking customers to provide honest reviews. Always avoid the temptation to review your own business or asking employees and friends to say nice things about you, since these artificial reviews tend to get identified removed quickly.

Analyzing competitors

One other frequently overlooked source of backlinks is competitor sites. Looking at sites in the same industry that regularly appear in searches for the keywords you are targeting can help undercover sources of inbound links you may have overlooked. There are several ways to do this, two of my favorites being:

- **Use Google**: search for the term `link:http://mycompetitor.com`, replacing the URL with your competitor's site name. This returns a list of all the sites providing a link to the URL (you can enter a page instead of the top-level domain name). You can manually check the PageRank of each source to find the relevant links that could help your site.

- **Use SEO SpyGlass from http://link-assistant.com**: there are both free and paid versions of this software, which automates checking competitor sites for backlinks (and determining their PageRank and link relevance). Apart from checking most major search engines, the resulting report (see next page) can provide invaluable insight into finding the top dozen or so links that your site can benefit from.

Competitor sites are a potential gold mine for sources of inbound links. If you're planning to outrank your competitors in SERPs, it's important to understand who is linking to them currently - your site should strive to have links that are higher in quality and quantity that their's.

Unfortunately, link building isn't a once-off procedure. When your site finally outranks others in your industry, you will need to continually scour the web for more sources for links. This is one of the major reasons for adding a blog to your site (see tip 15), since regularly high quality blog posts provide the easiest way to attract inbound links without having to manually request them.

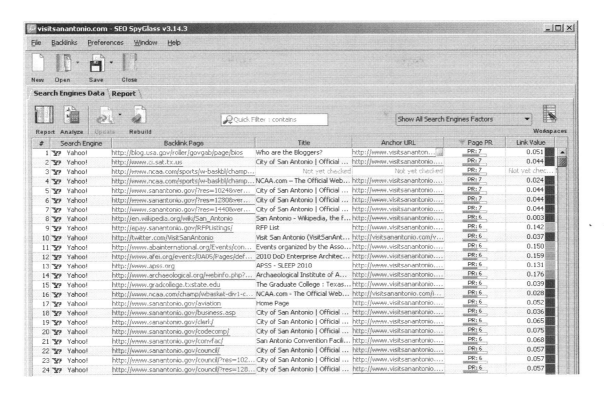

Don't Link to Bad Neighborhoods

Google calls spamming sites 'bad neighborhoods', and linking to them has a negative effect on both your PageRank and search engine rankings in general. While you cannot control inbound links from bad neighborhoods, which might happen over time, make sure you are not creating outbound links to those sites. To check the quality of a site, simply visit it - web pages with hundreds or thousands of links are not there to create content and you shouldn't link to these.

Link farms should also be avoided since they create large numbers of inbound links from low quality sites and can have a negative impact on your site's reputation with search engines. There are many services for providing link exchanges and, generally speaking, you should avoid these but if you *really* want to try one out, thoroughly vet their methodology and client base (I've yet to find one that works). All you have is your reputation, so don't damage it by associating with spammers.

For more on developing inbound links and 101 ways to build link popularity, visit http://www.seobook.com/archives/001792.shtml.

32 **Superlinks: .gov and .edu**

There are two types of quality inbound link that trump the rest: those from government and educational sites.

Though unconfirmed by Google, it's widely believed that inbound links coming from educational and government sites carry more credibility than those from other domain extensions. Any outbound link from a governmental or educational site to your site receives more credit than it would do from a regular website, though how much more credit is unclear. You should still focus on the quality pages within those sites (such as department sites rather than students' home pages) and work on getting links from those pages to your site.

How do you get an inbound link from a .gov or .edu site? There are a variety of methods:

- **Check your customer list:** if you supply a governmental or educational body, see if they have a website ending in the official extension. If so, politely request that you can be added to a vendor list or any page where it may be appropriate.

- **Check for blogs you can comment on**: these sites often have blogs just like most other quality sites, so find blog posts discussing your topics of expertise and contribute a relevant, useful comment with a link back to your site.

- **Check for forums you can participate in**: as above, find a thread that you can make a valid contribution to, and make sure to include your link.

- **Offer and promote your services**: if your business specializes in services that could be useful to a school or government agency, approach them with discounted rates, free advice, classes, events or guest lectures that can be traded for a link. If you have a hotel next to a university, provide a special rate available through a link on their website.

- **Review their programs or services**: if a school offers programs that are related to your business (eg. LEED consulting for construction businesses, or marketing programs for advertising agencies), publish a review and request a link from their website administrator. For government agencies, if you have a positive review about their performance and appreciate their work, request a link in the same way.

- **Donate money**: if your business donates money to a school (or charity sponsored by a government agency), or has an ongoing participation in charitable activities, ask if they would be willing to include your URL and name on a relevant page.

As with any organization, government and educational sites like positive press as much as anyone else - it's surprising how much good reviews are appreciated, and how quickly a link to your site can be generated based upon this alone. Aside from reviews, many .gov and .edu sites produce white papers and research that impact your business, and it's likely that at least one of these sites has generated content that's relevant to your industry.

Blogs and forums

If you decide to take part in the blogs and forums on these sites, I cannot emphasize enough how important it is to contribute positively in the comments and forums to gain the benefit here. The blogs and forums will be vigorously monitored and any commercial contributions appearing to be self-promotional or spam will get deleted rapidly. If your site is covered with advertising, it's also likely that your link won't last long.

Before you even attempt these tactics, review your site to ensure that you're offering web pages that are high quality and relevant otherwise their links won't last long. In other tips, I've discussed how blog posts, white papers and content related to industry-specific news will elevate your site's relevance to your audience - this is especially true of *this* audience.

Since .edu and .gov sites aren't always the most prominent in general search results, you can use Google's search engine operators to provide results related *only* to these sites. Open a browser, navigate to **http://google.com** and use these search phrases:

- Educational (general): search **site:.edu "keyword"**.
- Educational forum: search **site:.edu inurl:forum "keyword"**.
- Educational blog: search **site:.edu inurl:blog "keyword"**.
- Governmental (general): search **site:.gov "keyword"**
- Governmental forum: search **site:.gov inurl:forum "keyword"**
- Governmental blog: search **site:.gov inurl:blog "keyword"**

These search operators restrict results to sites with the specified extension, for blog or forum pages exclusively that contain the keyword or keyword phrase you are interested in.

If you find that your products or services are not well represented here, another method is to search for competitors instead of keywords. Logically, if a government or educational blog is willing to show a link to a competitor, it's likely that you can squeeze your link in there too, or at the very least work out how your competitor managed to get the link.

33 Use Press Releases

Press releases combine a great way to spread the word about your product or service together with the need for fresh and relevant content to boost rankings.

The basic principle of most search engines is to provide timely and relevant content to their users. By definition this means that regularly changing content and new information has an advantage over static pages. Small and medium-sized organizations tend to under-use the news tools available, and generating a press release can be both surprisingly easy and effective for SEO.

Many clients wrongly assume that there isn't much newsworthy happening in their company, but there are always events that can be a gold mine for information, such as:

- New products, services, promotions and programs.
- Completion of projects, milestones or announcements of contracts or new partnerships.
- New personnel, establishing offices or winning awards.
- Releasing industry white-papers, eBooks or interviews with company personnel.

Newsworthiness is important, however - the job of the press release is to broadcast interesting information that will grab attention. When writing your press release, remember that you're not writing ad copy, so temper the self-promotion with genuinely useful information and insight.

Unlike traditional press releases that were primarily written for journalists, most releases today will be read directly by the end user (as well as other media). Write the piece as if you are a journalist - use quotes from people involved, including customers if appropriate, and keep the language in the third person (e.g."ABC announced today that..." rather than "We announced today"). You should emulate the qualities that make good journalism by getting your point across quickly, double-checking your spelling and grammar and making sure that if the copy was duplicated by the newspaper word-for-word, it would sound professional.

A well-written press release will generate backlinks from quality news sites, improve your ranking in search engines, potentially create media attention as well as a significant spike in traffic to your site. You have the ability to reach customers, journalists, bloggers and others in your industry, so it pays to study and emulate the style of popular press releases and use distribution sites to get your message broadly disseminated.

Elements of a Press Release

- **Titles** and headlines provide the hook to pique readers' interest. Poor headlines, like bad movie titles, don't attract an audience, so choose a few words that will make people want to read more. And don't forget to use your keywords, since titles have more SEO emphasis than copy!

- **Summary**: while your press release may be several paragraphs, create a brief summary that states a problem and solution or some benefit for the reader.

- **Body**: include several links to internal pages of your site or relevant third-party pages, and use images and video where possible. It's important to get the main point across in the first paragraph and avoid complicated or overly technical language that will lose the reader. You should not include a date - at the breakneck speed of Internet news, your article may seem dated.

- **Company information**: this should read like the "elevator speech" for your company and give a good idea of what your company's history, skills and capabilities are.

- **Press contact**: while this may sound obvious, it's essential to include the email, phone number and name of the person who can verify the story or provide more information.

Distribution sites

In additional to the variety of free and paid distribution sites, don't forget to place the text of the press release on your own site. Some of the most popular PR sites include:

- http://www.prweb.com/
- http://www.prnewswire.com/
- http://www.clickpress.com/
- http://www.24-7pressrelease.com/
- http://www.businesswire.com/
- http://www.przoom.com/
- http://www.prleap.com/
- http://www.marketwire.com/

While these sites provide significant reach for your news, don't neglect your own distribution network through Twitter, Facebook and other social media sites and also email subscribers. In summary, find something newsworthy, write about it succinctly and professionally, and push to the press release to as many people as possible.

34 **Social bookmarking**

Sharing bookmarks helps good content rise to top. But one man's bookmark is another's inbound link.

In the quest for quality inbound links, it's easy to overlook social bookmarking sites which enable users to share bookmarks with their friend network. These sites evolved from the need to keep track of bookmarks from any computer connected to the web, rather than having the bookmarks tied to one specific computer or browser.

When users add a bookmark, rather than the site just collecting the URL and site title, most social bookmarking tools allow the user to tag the type of content and provide a description (see right). In the case of StumbleUpon, one of the most popular sites, this information is used to provide recommendations to other users who have stated an interest in a given topic.

Social bookmarking has two immediate advantages:

- The bookmarks themselves become a source of traffic to your site, independent of direct or search engine visitors, and represent an additional channel for the promotion of content.

- The categorization and description is likely used by many search engines to understand the content of the web page, and the bookmark effectively becomes a free inbound link with strong anchor text (see tip 29).

Additionally, if pages are bookmarked by many users, they become recommended more often, which in turn leads to more bookmarking. With each bookmark acting almost like a vote of approval, it's possible for a page to "go viral" and attract large numbers of visitors.

There are two main ways to take advantage of this:

- **Submit yourself**: sign up for an account with each service and submit every valuable page of your site. Remember, indexes are page-based so don't just add the top-level URL (e.g. http://test.com) but add deep links. It's not necessary to include content such as privacy policies.

- **Get others to submit your pages**: add a social bookmarking 'widget' to each page in your site (see tip 30), allowing visitors to quickly recommend the page if they like your content.

The first method can be time-consuming and may have limited impact, since your single vote will only have a limited influence on the popularity of a page. Increasingly it's frowned upon to submit your own content despite being extremely common. The second method can be highly effective if

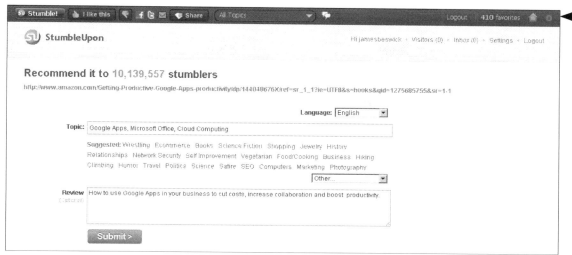

you have well designed, popular pages. Since third-party visitors are bookmarking the content, and as more 'votes' are counted the more the page is promoted within the social bookmarking sites as popular. (Popularity breeds popularity in social media.)

There are many examples of pages becoming successful through social bookmarking, and while your pages may not have the popularity of viral legends like *Will It Blend?* (**http://willitblend.com**), it's not difficult to generate a steady stream of traffic from these sites.

Generally speaking, the following types of content tend to be the most popular in social bookmarking:

- Guides (e.g. "Plan your trip to Italy")
- Tutorials: pages providing step-by-step advice on how to do something (e.g. "How to replace a broken window").
- Lists (e.g. "Top 10 Tips for Buying a New Car")
- Topical, funny or entertaining media - (e.g. *Lolcats*).

For more information, read "The Social Media Marketing Book" by Dan Zarella.

The most popular social bookmarking sites include:

- Bebo
- BookmarkSync
- Del.icio.us
- Digg
- Faves
- Google Bookmarks
- Ma.gnolia
- Mixx
- Newsvine
- Reddit
- StumbleUpon
- TechNet
- Twitter
- Windows Live Favorites
- Yahoo Bookmarks

35 **Sign up for Twitter. Start Tweeting**

Twitter is a major force in micro-blogging and real-time updates and should be part of your SEO strategy.

Twitter is a deceptively simple service that allows individuals and businesses to send short updates to their followers. The 140-character limit is ideal for posting links to industry or company news, providing updates about special offers, or engaging your audience in conversation. The concept has been so successful that Twitter has become a form of 'micro-blogging', enabling users to provide brief snippets of content in a format that's easier to write and faster to consume than full-length blogging.

Rather than simply providing a layer of chatter in addition to other social media networks, it can become a significant tool in your SEO strategy. Since one of the major goals of SEO is reaching the first page of search page results, when Google started including real-time Tweets in a prominent place on that first page, it effectively sanctioned Twitter as a new and powerful weapon in SEO. Tweeting about trending topics provides a simple albeit brief placement on page one of Google:

Searching on a hashtag shows realtime tweets for that topic.

Signing up for Twitter

The first step is to check that your brand name hasn't been taken - log into **http://twitter.com** to ensure that your desired user name is still available. Ideally, your Twitter name should match your brand name exactly (eg. One Uproar's ID is @oneuproar), since Google only currently pulls precise matches in their search results.

If you find that your name has already been claimed, you can file a trademark squatting complaint and attempt to reclaim the ID (be warned, however, this is mainly successful for broadly recognized brands rather than small businesses). See **http://help.twitter.com/entries/15789-how-to-file-terms-of-service-or-rules-complaints** for details on how to file a complaint.

Within your Twitter profile, there are several parts that are important to complete as fully as possible in order to create a professional Twitter 'presence' and attract followers (see the profile above):

- **Name**: the full name of your organization or business with main keywords included.

- **Location**: for most businesses, location is relevant for customers, and this helps search engines determine geographic relevance for your Tweets.

- **Website**: also this URL is 'no-followed', meaning it doesn't provide any meaningful inbound link to your main site, you should include this as a convenience for visitors.

- **Bio**: a description of your organization, including the major keyword phrases that would allow your profile to be discovered. Since potential followers search for other Twitter users to follow, your biography is important in attracting interest in your topics

- **Profile picture**: a small, square graphic that's either a photo of the person Tweeting, or a version of the corporate logo - this appears wherever your Tweets are shown both on Twitter.com and the third-party tools available.

- **Background graphic**: a full-page graphic appearing in the background of your main Twitter page (visible at http://twitter.com/*yourtwitterusername*), which can be used to create a more polished look for your profile.

You can change any of these at any time, so you should experiment with a variety of keyword phrases and graphics to find the most successful combination for building a list of followers.

Building Followers

Perhaps the most frustrating and confusing part of starting a new Twitter account is finding followers, since you have to convince other people to take action to follow you. Unlike email lists, which many companies still purchase or simply harvest from business cards, there's no direct distribution in Twitter beyond others who have decided to 'tune-in' to your Tweets.

The main steps here are:

- **Search for Twitter profiles** with interests that align to your business, and follow those profiles. Ideally find profiles that are actively Tweeting, since inactive accounts are unlikely to follow you back or be listening to your updates.

- **See which competitors** have a Twitter account and follow their followers in the hopes they may follow you back. Followers of competitors likely have interests that make your profile useful to them.

- **Promote your Twitter page** online on your web page by embedding widgets to show your latest Tweets. Also ensure that your Twitter ID is added in email signatures and newsletters.

- **Promote your page offline** in any printed stationery (invoices, business cards, etc.), newspaper and magazine advertising and flyers.

- **Create promotions** to encourage clients and potential customers to follow you on Twitter - companies such as Dell and Overstock.com do an excellent job of providing one-of-a-kind deals to encourage an active following.

While there is software available that will auto-follow large numbers of profiles to accelerate the number that follow you back, overly-aggressive use of these will get your ID banned. In the long run, it's better to build a Twitter base slowly and surely, since you'll end up with higher quality followers (i.e. a real person interested in your updates, rather than bots, spammers and aggregators).

Twitter tips

Many major search engines are taking steps to include tweets in their page one search results, and since much of SEO is about reaching the first page, in many respects a well-managed Twitter account can achieve more than many other tactics combined:

- **Use hashtags**: one of the easiest ways to get your tweets out to non-followers is through the intelligent use of hashtags (like this: #sports), which act as categories for your tweets. Look at what your competitors and industry tweets about, and which hashtags they use for an idea of what topics are being discussed and searched for.

- **Tweet links to new site content**: when you post new content to your site, make sure to tweet out the update. Not everyone is watching your site for changes, so a polite tweet can drive new traffic to your web pages.

- **Retweet** content from your followers that reinforces your brand, keywords, products and services - place 'RT' in front of another user's message to retweet. Also engage in responses to your messages, since Twitter is more of a dialog than a one-way marketing platform.

- **Shrink your links** with URL shorteners like bit.ly, is.gd or su.pr. These compress the URLs, allowing you to fit more text into each Tweet, and many provide tracking services to measure how many of your followers click the link.

- **Provide newsworthy information**: Twitter is about real-time timely news, so make sure your messages reward your followers by staying on-topic, relevant and interesting.

While it can take time to build a loyal and interactive Twitter fan base, perseverance and consistency pays off. Over time tweets can provide a steady stream of traffic to your website, and well as an additional presence in the first page of search results.

36 Build a Facebook page

Facebook is a huge platform with a loyal following - make your official page a social media hub.

If you thought Facebook was MySpace for 20-somethings, think again. With 400 million active users, 50% of which log in every day, Facebook is a virtual country that can help you communicate with your customers and grow your brand. Although Facebook only allows *real* people to join, companies are represented with official pages that Facebook users can join as fans (similar to Twitter followers). As with Twitter, your fans elect to follow you, so news and updates are consumed by an audience that has an interest in your business.

Building a page takes minutes - building the fan base is a longer project. There are currently around 1.5 million local businesses on Facebook, and you can join by visiting **http://www.facebook.com/pages/create.php** (shown opposite). Simply select your business category and name, agree to the terms and conditions and click Create to set up your page. With the default page in place, you should modify the following to build a basic page:

- **Settings** (under Edit Page): set Country and Age restrictions, if appropriate.
- **Info tab**: add your physical location, opening hours, contact details, website link and profile.
- **Home page:** add your company logo or - better still, a compelling image related to your business - and general description (including your website).

There are additional tabs enabling fans to upload photos, write reviews and take part in discussions - since the goal is to engage your audience, you should leave these features activated.

How to use your Facebook page

The Facebook page provides another channel to publish blog posts, site updates, special offers, coupons, company news, events and media such as photos and video. Content can be added to the news feed using the Share box at the top of the screen - once published, it appears in your fans' news feed. The goal is to provide fans with content that adds value to their feed.

The most effective fan pages also become resources for their fans, providing guides and information that make the page a destination in itself. For example, hotels can provide city guides and travel advice for visitors, and retailers can publish buyers guides and insight into their products. This can be especially effective in the business-to-business market (B2B), enabling your company provide value to

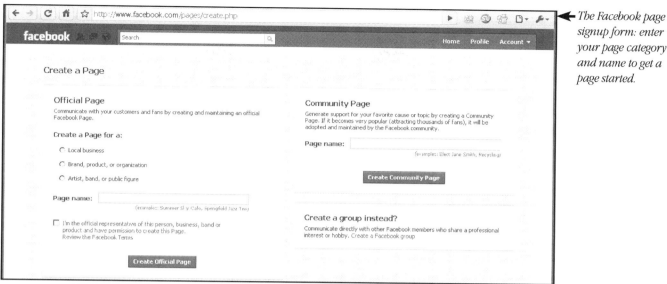

The Facebook page signup form: enter your page category and name to get a page started.

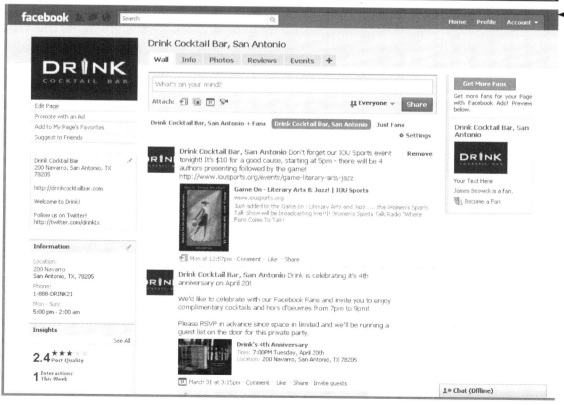

A completed Facebook fan page, showing company news, events and blog updates.

existing customers and reaching out to a new companies that don't already know about your business. Once your page is ready and you start to publish content and see fans subscribing:

- **Connect to Twitter**: go to **http://www.facebook.com/twitter** to link your page with your Twitter account - this will push updates to your Twitter newsfeed, automating the extra step of publishing on both platforms.

- **Claim your username**: although you have to build a body of fans and activity first, once established you can claim a globally unique username at **http://www.facebook.com/username** which will replace the long page URL you are initially given.

As with blog posts and Tweets, you should ensure that your posts are newsworthy and relevant and not so frequent as to irritate your audience. By coordinating Facebook, Twitter and blogging, your posts can be pushed to an audience of subscribers that will help to build your following over time.

As a fan page administrator, you have access to the Insights panel of your page, which you should monitor regularly This shows the demographic of your fans, their level of interaction, the number of new or leaving fans and a range of other metrics.

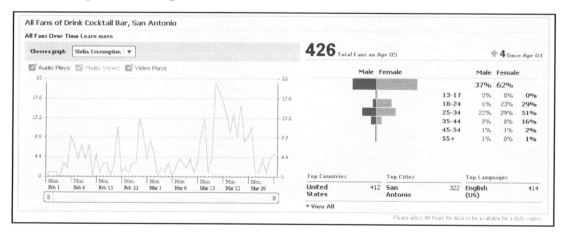

Finding fans organically

Finding fans takes time and effort - there are several ways to do this organically (without cost):

- **Your network**: invite your colleagues, vendors and customers to join your page, either through email. This should provide an initial body of fans to get the page started. Getting employees to contribute to the social media effort by developing their own content will spur them to develop an audience - which then becomes your audience.

- **Link to your page**: show the Facebook logo on your website to encourage click-throughs, and including the URL in marketing materials and offline stationary such as business cards, brochures, menus and newspaper advertising. Funnel visitors from other channels to Facebook, since activity on other channels is one of fastest ways to build fans from existing contacts.

- **Offer an incentive**: publish coupons, special offers and weekly deals only available to Facebook fans. Although it's technically difficult to ensure these are only used by the fans, incentives are an effective way to build the fan base.

While organic growth is time-consuming, it eventually produces a network of quality fans: namely people who have an interest in your business, even if the subscriber base is small.

Ideas for your Facebook page

Facebook provides a unique ability for brands to connect with their audience: many larger companies have built successful pages with millions of fans. Although we're starting small, here are some of the best ideas for making your Facebook page a social media hub for your brand.

- **Be creative with your page image**: although you can just upload your logo, there are some creative 'hacks' that will make your picture stand out. For ideas, there's an excellent tutorial at **http://www.allfacebook.com/2009/02/facebook-profile-photo-hacks**.

- **Use applications**: there are over a half million Facebook applications, which are programs built on the Facebook platform, and many of these can be built into your fan page with relatively little effort. These help create a more engaging experience for the user, making them stay on your page for longer and return more frequently. Many larger brands have built successful proprietary applications, one of the most famous being Burger King's *Whopper Sacrifice* application.

- **Remember, it's a two-way dialog**. Social media is about entering the conversation that's happening with your customers, rather than selling products. Every time somebody comments, adds photos or interacts with your page, you need to comment back and respond. Fans lose interest if the company doesn't respond, whereas their opinion of your brand improves when you do.

- **Post and tag users in photos**: as you start to add media to your page, include people (with their permission). Photos of co-workers and customers provide a more personal side to your business than pictures of your products. The more tagged photos you generate, the more popular your page will become.

- **Events**: if you host seminars, webinars, parties or any other type of event, list it on Facebook. As the event becomes more popular, it starts to gain momentum in the news feed of your fans.

37 Facebook advertising

Targeted advertising on the world's biggest social network is one of the easiest ways to build traffic.

Much like search engine marketing, advertising on Facebook allows marketers to work with a budget of any size and create, modify or cancel ads in real-time. If a given advert is not working, it can be changed or deleted immediately, and the real-time statistics provide a comprehensive view of the number of impressions, clicks and the click-through rate for any part of your campaign. Facebook also offers one major benefit that has no comparison in search engine marketing - the ads can be targeted with demographic precision.

Create a range of demographically targeted ads and be guided by the click-through rate and cost per click.

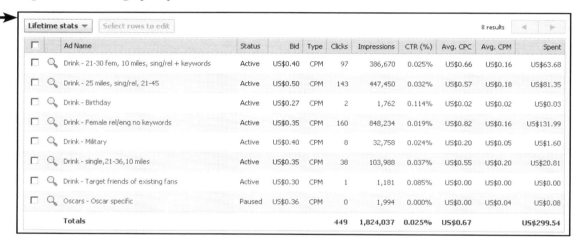

	Ad Name	Status	Bid	Type	Clicks	Impressions	CTR (%)	Avg. CPC	Avg. CPM	Spent
	Drink - 21-30 fem, 10 miles, sing/rel + keywords	Active	US$0.40	CPM	97	386,670	0.025%	US$0.66	US$0.16	US$63.68
	Drink - 25 miles, sing/rel, 21-45	Active	US$0.50	CPM	143	447,450	0.032%	US$0.57	US$0.18	US$81.35
	Drink - Birthday	Active	US$0.27	CPM	2	1,762	0.114%	US$0.02	US$0.02	US$0.03
	Drink - Female rel/eng no keywords	Active	US$0.35	CPM	160	848,234	0.019%	US$0.82	US$0.16	US$131.99
	Drink - Military	Active	US$0.40	CPM	8	32,758	0.024%	US$0.20	US$0.05	US$1.60
	Drink - single,21-36,10 miles	Active	US$0.35	CPM	38	103,988	0.037%	US$0.55	US$0.20	US$20.81
	Drink - Target friends of existing fans	Active	US$0.30	CPM	1	1,181	0.085%	US$0.00	US$0.00	US$0.00
	Oscars - Oscar specific	Paused	US$0.36	CPM	0	1,994	0.000%	US$0.00	US$0.04	US$0.08
	Totals				449	1,824,037	0.025%	US$0.67		US$299.54

Relevancy + Targeted Demographic = Lower cost per click

While Google AdWords can be a great marketing platform when it's executed effectively, fundamentally it's difficult to know very much about the demographic viewing your ads. You can fine tune with geography, day-parting, and niche keyword phrasing, but there's no information showing if an ad is being seen by a 55-year old man on his home computer or his 18-year old daughter who shares it.

What Facebook brings to the table, apart from an enormous and active audience, is the profile demographic before your ad is shown. We've consistently seen the same effects as ads are fine-tuned based upon demographics, and the results are good news for marketers — well-written ads that are targeted appropriately absolutely lower the cost per click.

Developing an ad for Facebook: first, build your ad headline and copy.

In the second step, enter the geographic and demographic targets.

119

When crafting your ad, there are a variety of demographic metrics which you can use to narrow down the number of potential people who will see it (see previous page). As you change these, keep a watchful eye on the Estimated Reach and campaign cost at the bottom:

The ad on the previous page will be seen by an estimated 435,700 people who meet the demographic profile.

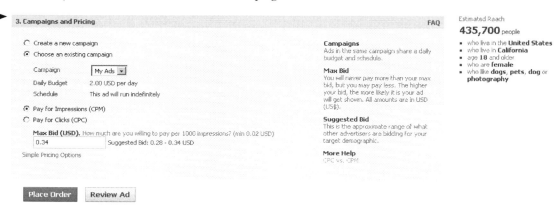

- **CPC or CPM**: You have a choice of paying by click (CPC) or per 1,000 impressions (CPM). A good strategy is to start with broad ads on CPM and then create more targeted ads using CPC for the best impact. In other words, create a campaign to everyone broadly, and after 100,000 impressions use the insights to see who clicked the ad. If the results showed 25-30 year-old married females were responsible for the most clicks, rewrite the ad with that demographic in mind, and reset as a CPC campaign.

- **Segmentation**: demographics enable fine segmentation of your ads. Why push one Valentine's Day ad to everyone, when you could create dozens appealing to different age groups, genders, and relationship statuses? The more finely segmented the ad, the better the click-through rate, and it's easy to build multiple versions of ads for a given campaign.

The ad can promote your Facebook page but it's not the only possible target: it can link to external landing pages too. Generally speaking, we've found fan pages to be highly successful for B2C business – especially those such as hotels, restaurants, bars and retail – and landing pages better suited to B2B products, but it's still worth experimenting for your particular market.

Birthdays are a special option in Facebook ads, enabling users to see an ad only on their birthday. Generally these ads have a high CPC yet lower CPM, and a low click rate. But when clicks occur, these are highly targeted and can be easily to convert (e.g. "Our birthday gift to you").

Use the 'Always Be Testing' mantra to fine-tune your ad copy and demographics – the results can be substantially lower cost-per-clicks compared with SEM.

Targeting factors

Targeting by demographic is almost an SEM dream come true, but it also takes some fine-tuning. There is a natural skew in the Facebook user base that's younger than the national average, with females being more active than males. Also, this is based on user-reported data not the Census, so some degree of 'misstating the facts' occurs, including misrepresenting age, college education, relationship status and interests.

As you modify these factors, Facebook provides an estimate of the number of people who might see the ad (see left). It's easy to get carried away with the large audience that seemed to escape your previous marketing efforts, but I would suggest the following:

- **Start small**: you will often get the best results when initially targeting an ad to an audience of 10,000-25,000 people. The feedback metrics will help keep the campaign cost under control when the ads are scaled to larger numbers of viewers.

- **Cap your daily budget**: the overall cap will cause the campaign to stop intraday as soon as a dollar value is reached - this is a great safety measure.

- **Use the network**: click-through rates are often higher when you target friends of connections, even though the number of impressions will be lower - friends trust fan pages and products that other friends are connected with.

- **Exercise those keywords**: since Facebook updates the estimate as keywords are added, it's very easy to see how many people have expressed an interest directly in a given topic.

- **Different languages**: profiles indicate a user's first language – it's inexpensive to get ads translated to languages other than English, and frequently the CTR can be higher, simply because so many advertisers neglect customers whose first language isn't English.

Once you have campaigns running, keep monitoring the dashboard and look at the profile of people who have clicked your ads. If you're attracting the wrong customer base (e.g. fans from New York for a zoo in Seattle), tweak the ad to exclude wasted clicks. And don't forget that while clicks and fans are great, the ultimate target is to generate conversions - make sure your landing pages have compelling content and effectively funnel traffic towards your end goal. A low-cost, high CTR looks good on paper, but you have to measure the ROI.

Facebook provides more best practices for advertising at http://www.facebook. com/ads/best_practices.php.

38 Get listed on Google Local Business

Google's local listings are often listed on the first page of results and can become a major source of for traffic.

It's no secret that Google is starting to look at an ever-increasing number of off-page factors, most of which are hard to control from an SEO perspective, in order to rank pages. So when there are off-page elements that are completely within our control, they should be the among the first tasks in getting a site ready for page one prime-time.

Google Local Business Center is one of those factors, and is the driver behind Google Maps – if you have a organization where the physical location is important to your customers (eg. gyms, jewelry stores, retail, etc.) you should take full advantage of your Local Business Center listing. You may find you already have a skeleton listing, but adding rich content to your profile will help to bring visitors to your site - and place of business.

There are several areas of interest from an SEO point of view:

- **Map searches** are a major source of traffic for sites – anywhere between 10-30% is not unusual. Ensuring a thorough listing gives you the best opportunity of funneling visitors to your site.

- **Rich information** can be embedded, including business description, opening hours, coupons, business photos and aggregated reviews from other sites.

- **Mobile users** are big consumers of these listings since the results are geared towards location-based relevance.

- **Keyword analysis** shows how visitors found your listing, and quite often will reveal keyword phrases you may have overlooked on your website and landing pages.

Although this tip is geared towards Google's service, the other major search engines offer similar applications that you should also participate in. Sign-up for this free service, and the ones offered by Yahoo! and Micrsoft Bing here:

- Google: **http://google.com/localbusinesscenter**.
- Yahoo! Local: **http://local.yahoo.com**.
- Microsoft Bing Local Listings: **https://ssl.bing.com/listings**.

You will need to verify ownership and accuracy of the data provided: Google provides a YouTube video to walk you through the process: **http://www.youtube.com/watch?v=W11DCs2CjlE** .

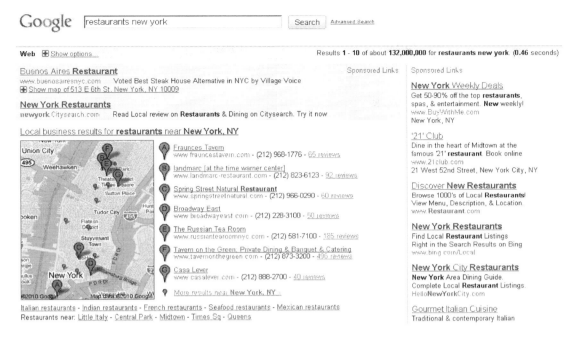

Aside from the obviously-welcome free traffic boost, and the factor that most of your competitors will have missed the opportunity giving you primary placement advantage on most map services, appearing here is a great way to reach mobile users.

While mobile traffic is still a tiny overall percentage, the growth in smart devices means that they will become much more significant in the near future. This is especially true for navigational applications and anything location-specific, as customers use their phones to find businesses in a way that didn't happen in the desktop environment.

Important parts of your listing

In addition to the basic details about your business, you should also include:

- A keyword-rich description, to ensure your listing appears for those searches.

- Hours of operation, payment options, parking information and relevant links.

- Photos and video.

- Coupons and special offers that enable you to identify the listing when a visit converts into a sale. Also ensure you also keep these offers refreshed regularly.

Interpreting the results

As with any other part of SEO, measuring performance and making adjustments is an essential part of retaining your top placement in the search results. Fortunately, Google Local Business Center provides comprehensive analytics that can help you improve your listing and understand how the traffic is being generated (see the analytics screen capture opposite).

1. Activity

The top graph shows the number of *impressions* - that is, the number of times your listing has appeared in search results - and the number of actions, meaning how of those impressions led to additional actions by the user. If you modify the start and end date range above, it's possible to see any seasonality affecting this channel's traffic.

2. Totals

Apart from the aggregate number of impressions, this breaks down the actions into a direct click through to your web site, asking for driving directions and selecting "More info" (which shows the additional rich content for your listing).

3. Top Search Queries

The report shows the top 10 search queries that caused your listing to appear. Due to relativity few listings having complete business information, and the geographic restriction of the search, it's common to find that your site is matching for broad search terms (one or two words) that would otherwise be difficult to rank for in the regular search results. If you find search terms here that are not currently targeted by your website, you should review these for appropriateness and traffic volume and consider amending your targeted keyword list.

4. Where driving requests originate from

This information can sometimes reveal visitors from cities that you are not currently targeting in both your online and offline advertising. It may also show that, if your location is hard to find, you should provide more detailed directions for visitors on your website.

Once your local listing is active, you should check its accuracy regularly, update coupons and special offers regularly, and monitor the statistics for any major changes in traffic, top search queries and conversions.

| Settings | Help | Sign out | English (United States) |

Dashboard | Coupons

« Locations
Drink Cocktail Bar

Apply

1 Jan, 2010 — 31 Mar, 2010

last 7 days | last 30 days

Activity

● **Impressions** ● **Actions**

Jan 1, 201 Jan 8, 201 Jan 15, 20 Jan 22, 2010

Totals

36952 impressions

How many times users saw your business listing as a local search result

966 actions

How many times users showed interest in your business listing

202 Clicks for more info on Maps
48 Clicks for driving directions
716 Clicks to your website

Top search queries

	Query	Impressions
1.	bars	8414
2.	nightlife	3364
3.	bar	3208
4.	coffee	2345
5.	restaurants	1948
6.	wine	1502
7.	coffee shops	1319
8.	wine bar	960
9.	coffee shop	915
10.	wine bars	794
	Other	12183

Where driving directions requests come from

	Region (by ZIP code)	Requests
1.	San Antonio 78205	20
2.	San Antonio 78204	4
3.	San Antonio 78251	4
4.	San Antonio 78216	3
5.	Austin 78701	2
6.	San Antonio 78223	2
7.	San Antonio 78229	2
8.	San Antonio 78255	2
9.	Driftwood 78619	1
10.	San Antonio 78210	1
	Other	7

Post to your place page View

Post about events, specials, and more.
Example: "Live music tonight at 7pm!"

Post

Expires in 30 days
160

Your business info ✎ Edit

100 % complete

200 Navarro
Suite 100
San Antonio, TX 78205
(210) 224-1031
http://drinkcocktailbar.com

Description: Over 200 brands of liquor, a signature cocktail menu with a range of draft beers. 4 large HD screens and daily Happy Hour from 5-7pm. Opposite the Hotel Contessa.
Payment: American Express, Cash, MasterCard, Visa
Average Price: $10
Speciality: Cocktails
Twitter: www.twitter.com/drinktx
Facebook: www.facebook.com/drinktx
Events: Bookable by arrangement
Bottle service: Available for premium liquor products
Email: info@drinkcocktailbar.com
Business Hours:
Monday: 5:00 pm - 2:00 am
Tuesday: 5:00 pm - 2:00 am
Wednesday: 5:00 pm - 2:00 am
Thursday: 5:00 pm - 2:00 am
Friday: 5:00 pm - 2:00 am
Saturday: 5:00 pm - 2:00 am
Sunday: 5:00 pm - 2:00 am
Categories: Bars, Nightlife, Cocktail Bar, Bar, Happy Hour

1 of 7 photos Next

Delete this listing

Improve your listing

- Creating a great listing
- Tips to help users find your business
- Business listing quality guidelines

Do you have more businesses?

✚ Add another listing
✚ Upload a data file

39 Use LinkedIn to market your site

LinkedIn provides an opportunity to market your expertise, and a valuable source for qualified traffic.

Unlike Facebook or Twitter, LinkedIn is a network of people's business and professional relationships, and can be a great platform for building your professional credibility and website traffic. Membership is free, and creating an account takes minutes, though cultivating a list a contacts takes longer. As with other social networks, it provides another channel for distributing site content and generating inbound links, but unlike the others offers unparalleled access to a community of highly qualified traffic that's directly related to your industry. Once you have created a basic accounts, follow these tips for increasing exposure and creating traffic.

Provide your business profile

Iin addition to your individual profile, LinkedIn also allows business pages for listing your organization. Here you can provide more information about your company and links to your site. You should also invite other employees in your firm to ensure their company appears in their individual profiles.

Answer questions

LinkedIn has a popular Q&A section accessible at **http://linkedin.com/answers**, similar to Yahoo! Answers. Apart from acting as an informal and rapid way to get information from the community, it offers an effective way to showcase your expertise and company services.

If you take the time to regularly contribute accurate and useful information, you can build credibility as a subject matter expert and drive traffic back to your site. Be sure to include URLs to relevant content on your site rather than just including a link to your domain arbitrarily.

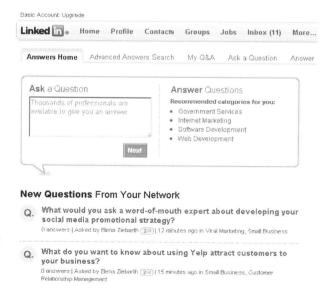

Grow your connections

Internally, LinkedIn is a friendship tree of professional connections. Once you have added your colleagues, co-workers, vendors and customers, you can explore their connections to build your network of contacts. You can also search by topic to find contacts, though you must use this judiciously and put time into developing relationships rather than spamming with the intent to create valueless connections.

Ask for recommendations

Don't be afraid to ask for a recommendation from people you have had a good working relationship with. Remarkably few members have more than a couple of recommendations, and having these will make your profile stand out and provide credibility.

Network Activity

This is LinkedIn's version of the Facebook status update, and provides another channel to market blog posts and content updates from your main site. By using a URL shortening service such as **http://bit.ly** or **http://su.pr**, you can uniquely track traffic resulting from Network Activity clicks. Network activity updates appear in your contacts' news feeds and in the weekly update email sent to your network.

Joining Groups

Join groups related to your industry or expertise by searching the directory at **http://www.linkedin.com/groups**.

After the group administrator approves your membership, you can then take part in discussions, post articles, and provide links back to content on your site.

The key to using LinkedIn successfully is in providing value to the community in order to gain gain exposure (and traffic) by contributing in a positive way and assisting their needs.

40 **Add your site to online directories**

While web directories are declining in importance, they still provide potential traffic sources and inbound links.

Web directories originated during the dawn of the Internet as a way to categorize sites and provide an index of all the content on the web. Directories are somewhat primitive compared to modern search engines, usually relying on human editors to approve submissions, restricting sites to a small number of categories, and treating entire domains as one entry rather than looking at each page.

There's much debate about whether directories have a role as the Internet develops, and how much weighting search engines such as Google give to these indexes. However, purely from an SEO perspective, it doesn't hurt your site's rankings and there are other benefits for websites to be included in these lists wherever possible:

- Your site may receive additional traffic from users of these directories - not everyone is using Google, Yahoo! and Bing to find results.

- Some directories have very high PageRank scores so your site's PR will benefit from the inbound links.

Adding your site to online directories is not the same thing as submitting to search engines, which is usually not necessary. For example, although there is a page called 'Submit URL to Google' (**http://www.google.com/addurl**), you don't need to do this. Providing there are inbound links to your pages from sites already in their index, Google will follow the trail and find your site without needing to be given the URL. It's somewhat counter-intuitive that Google should host its own submission page that has no effect, but adding your site to this page *does not* add you to the Google index, nor does it change the frequency in which the spiders return if you add the same site over and over.

How to add your site to the Open Directory Project

DMOZ, also known as the Open Directory Project, is the largest and oldest of online directories and has become less popular over the years as Google, Yahoo! and Wikipedia have encroached from either side. Unlike most search engines, DMOZ entries are managed manually by volunteer editors, and gaining entry relies on manual approval - which can be subjective and time-consuming.

To add your site to DMOZ, open a browser and go to **http://dmoz.org** - from here, use either the search field or tree of subjects to find the category that most closely describes your site. It's essential that the sub-category is as specific as possible to avoid rejection of your submission. You may find the most appropriate category is nested 8 to 10 levels deep from the main page, and you should double-check other websites listed in the category to decided if it's suitable. From here, click 'Suggest URL' in the top right menu:

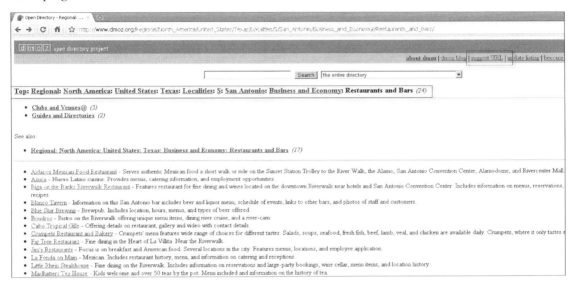

The submission form only consists of a few fields but it's important to follow the instructions closely. Don't submit multiple variations of the same URL (e.g. http://www.mysite.com and http://mysite.com), sites under construction or mirror sites, and ensure the description is an objective summary of the website rather than promotional text to attract visitors. For example:

- **A good description**: "Information about menus, special offers, opening hours and location of John Doe's burgers."

- **A bad description**: "John Doe's burgers are the best in Nebraska! Get your special burger offer by clicking here for an online burger discount expiring today!"

DMOZ is run by human editors who volunteer to manage thousands of submissions. By ensuring your entry helps maintain the integrity of their directory, you'll give your site the best opportunity to get indexed and the lowest chances of rejection. Also remember that acceptance to DMOZ can take months, so check back periodically to see if your site has become part of the index.

> If your submission is rejected, don't panic - DMOZ is just one directory in a long list of indexes and search engines.

Other online directories

DMOZ is a free directory, but most others charge a one-time processing or annual fee for inclusion. Here is a list of other directories worth considering, together with their pricing and PageRank scores as of June 2010:

- **Yahoo! Directory (http://dir.yahoo.com)**: this is the number two online directory, charging $299 per year for inclusion. PageRank 8.

- **ipl2 (http://www.ipl.org/)**: the merger of the Internet Public Library and Librarians' Internet Index, ipl2 offers free submission for sites that contain substantial content rather than purely commercial messages. PageRank 8.

- **Business Directory (http://www.business.com)**: charges $299 per year for a listing, with a primary focus on commercial web sites. Page Rank 7.

- **Wow Directory (http://www.wowdirectory.com)**: offers free or paid inclusion, and sposorship opportunities. PageRank 4.

- **Clush (http://www.clush.com/Dir)**: allows 5 URL submissions within the same domain for $20 a year, with a directory listing live in 24 hours. PageRank 6.

- **Starting Point Directory (http://www.stpt.com/directory)**: charges $99 per year for inclusion but doesn't accept blogs, other directories, sites with little original content or any sort of redirect or mirror sites. PageRank 4.

- **Gimpsy (http://www.gimpsy.com)**: this verb-based directory charges a one-time fee of $40 for a listing. PageRank 5.

- **JoeAnt (http://www.joeant.com)**: charges a one-time $40 fee, though listings are free for editors (anyone can sign up to become an editor). PageRank 5.

- **Web Beacon (http://web-beacon.com)**: originally based on GoGuides core data, a listing costs $40 though submissions are free for editors. PageRank 4.

- **Illumirate (http:// http://www.illumirate.com)**: similar to DMOZ, providing an editor-run free submission site. PageRank 5.

There are hundreds of other directories on the web, but considering the trade-off between listing fees and PageRank scores, I'd recommend the above sites in terms of value for money.

If you discover any other good directories, please feel free to email me for future editions of this book at **directories@ranking-number1.com**.

MORE SEO TECHNIQUES

In the final section of this book we examine a range of SEO tips outside the scope of the previous four parts.

Here we cover:

- Using Google Webmaster Tools and Google Analytics to gather results and fine-tune your site.
- Video as a new content medium for attracting visitors through YouTube and video search.
- Creating compelling email campaigns to drive more clicks to your landing pages and create repeat visitors.
- The myths surrounding social media and SEO.
- The benefits of creating affiliate programs for certain types of web site.
- Further resources for staying up-to-date with SEO trends, and how to get additional help.

Don't forget to visit the site's website at **http://ranking-number1.com** for additional resources!

41 Use Google Webmaster Tools

An invaluable free resource, GWT provides a range of information about how Google sees your site.

Google Webmaster Tools (GWT) provides a peek into how Google is viewing your site - it's Google-specific but does provide some information that apply to other engines too. The first step to getting your site analyzed is to sign up, which you can do at **http://www.google.com/webmasters/tools** using a Google Account (you can create one for free if you don't have one).

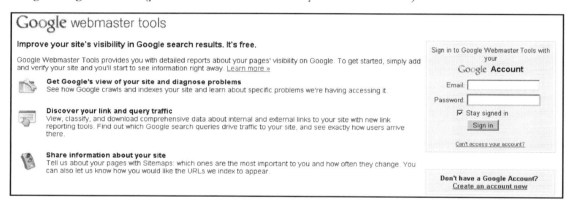

Once you are logged into GWT, the first step is to add your website to your profile. In order to do this, you have to show you have administrative rights over the website (which prevents users from randomly adding any site). Click "Add a site", enter your domain name and click "Continue".

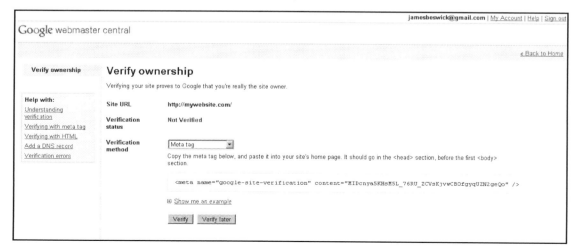

This leads to the ownership verification page, where you must complete one of three tasks:

- **Add a meta tag**: to do this, you need access to the source code of your home page (usually index.html). Simply copy and paste the text provided into the `<head>` section. This entry has no effect on the appearance of your site.

- **Add an HTML file** to your web server: first, download the HTML verification file provided. This file is empty but contains a specific name GWT is looking for. To upload the file to your web server, you need the FTP username and password to access the file system. One you have these, use an FTP client such as FileZilla (**http://FileZilla.com**) to copy the file to the public_html directory.

- **Add a DNS record**: you will need access to the domain name control panel at your domain registrar to add a TXT record with the random code provided. DNS records can take from several minutes to several hours to propagate throughout the Internet, so verification may take some time.

The method you choose will depend upon your level of access to your site and your technical knowledge: for most people, adding the HTML file is the simplest of the three, and the one least likely to lead to errors that cause site unavailability. Whichever you choose, click "Verify" after you have performed the steps and the site will appear on your GWT dashboard.

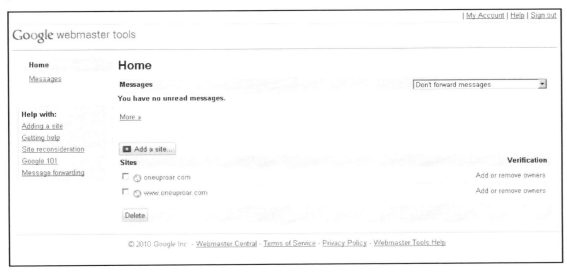

For more information on setting up GWT, visiting Google's help at http://www. google.com/support/webmasters.

Google Webmaster Tools has a number of useful features that help identify problems that may be preventing spiders from correctly viewing all your site's content.

Submit and check a site map

Once you have a sitemap available (see tip 20), select "Sitemaps" from the "Site Configuration" menu and click "Submit a Sitemap" to schedule Googlebot to read the file. This can take a while, and the status will show a green tick when completed. Clicking the sitemap's name will show any errors that were encountered - you can follow up on each of these and resubmit the file if necessary.

Checking crawler access

The robots.txt file provides search engines with directives to follow - or not follow - content on your site. Under "Site Configuration", click "Crawler access" to show what Googlebot finds here. The main reason to use robots.txt is to hide directories and content from search engines to avoid duplicate content issues. It's not designed as a security layer - if you need to protect content, you should use password based security and the webserver configuration to keep spiders and people away.

It's critical to make sure this file isn't blocking the entire website's content, and the "Test" tab enables you to check the visibility of files to Googlebot. Details about the syntax in this file can be found at **http://www.robotstxt.org**, but the most important part to check is that the file doesn't contain the syntax "Disallow: /" which will make all your content invisible.

The third tab enables requests for URL removal, specifically intended for removing private or old pages from appearing in the index. It's important to make sure you have read and complied with Google's removal requirements shown on the page before making this request.

Site configuration options

There are a handful of other site configuration options to optimize Googlebot's view of your website:

- **Change of address**: this section provides step-by-step instructions for managing the transition of a website from one domain name to another, including handling 301 redirects.

- **Geographic target**: if, like most sites, your business is mainly tied to one country and you have a neutral top-level domain (such as .com), use this feature to indicate your country of focus. Although you will appear less often in the search results for users outside your selected country, you will potentially receive more traffic from within the country you operate in.

- **Preferred domain**: indicate to Google whether you prefer you site to be shown with or without the www prefix (see tip 28 on canonical naming problems). If you select to remove www, you will have to add your site again to GWT using the non-www format.

- **Crawl rate**: this supposedly allows some control over the frequency of Googlebot visits, but I've yet to see any evidence that this setting has any effect. More usefully, the crawl stats indicate how many pages Googlebot views on a daily basis, together with the download time.

- **Sitelinks** are the navigational links that appear directly in Google's search results for the most popular sites. The vast majority of sites have no sitelinks available because Google's algorithm has determined there's not enough traffic. You have no control over whether Google decides to display sitelinks, but if they do you can make modifications here.

Using GWT for SEO

While there are a variety of features in GWT that any website owner should monitor frequently for changes, some of the most important (and overlooked) statistics have a major effect on how your site rank in Google's search results:

- **Crawler errors** indicate pages that are missing or unreachable, or where time-outs occurred (meaning the page took too long to load). These errors must be checked and handled regularly since 404 errors changing URLs can resulting in substantially lower rankings.

- **Keywords** shows a list of the most common keywords across the site, and should reflect the keywords you planned on using - if not, you must modify the content of your site.

- **Site performance** provides detailed information about how to improve the loading time for specific pages on your site. Implementing these suggestions can make a dramatic difference to the visitor experience, but may also have a reasonable impact on how Google ranks your site.

Since Google frequently changes the functionality of GWT, keep up to date by visiting their blog at http://googlewebmastercentral.blogspot.com/.

42 Set up Google Analytics

In hitting your SEO goals, measuring performance is the key to discovering what's working - or not.

Offline media has no counterpart to Google Analytics: when running a newspaper or magazine advertisement, there's not much feedback available about how many people saw it or responded to its call to action. The online world is almost the complete opposite, with a range of tools that track, analyze and report on the smallest of actions that visitors take.

Google Analytics is one of the best products available to this end - apart from being completely free, it's possible to build a rich picture of how visitors are behaving, which content is popular, and which pages are converting to sales. Analytics provides the glue that can improve the return on investment on your site. There are two important parts to Analytics: installation and monitoring.

Installing Google Analytics

The first step is to visit **http://google.com/analytics** and create an account. If you use other Google services such as Gmail, Analytics can be attached to this account, otherwise you will have to create a Google account first. Once you are logged in, simply enter the domain name of your website, and you will be provided with a small code snippet - Google Analytics is a script that runs on every single page of your site, enabling the service to collect data as visitors move from one page to another. The script looks like this:

```
<script type="text/javascript">
var gaJsHost = (("https:" == document.location.protocol) ?
"https://ssl." : "http://www.");
document.write(unescape("%3Cscript src='" + gaJsHost + "google-
analytics.com/ga.js' type='text/javascript'%3E%3C/script%3E"));
</script>
<script type="text/javascript">
try {
var pageTracker = _gat._getTracker("UA-XXXXXX-XX");
pageTracker._trackPageview();
} catch(err) {}</script>
```

The bold text above will be replaced with your user account identifier. The entire code block must be added to the HTML of your webpages just before the closing </body> tag.

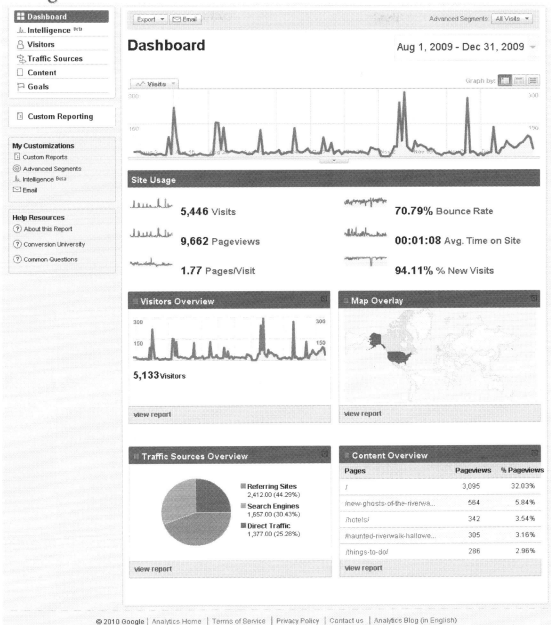

Google Analytics Features

Google Analytics collects data continuously though the reports are only updated every 24 hours. After logging in and selecting your site, the first screen is the Dashboard. The simple interface belies an extremely powerful reporting system capable of crunching a large amount of data. Covering every feature is well beyond the scope of this book, but here are the major areas.

Dashboard

The dashboard contents can be customized by dragging panels around or deleting them entirely. The default setup includes:

- **The date range,** which can be changed to show any period since Analytics starting collecting data for the site.

- **Visits**: measures the total number of visitors to the site each day. Clicking the drop-down allows you to graph one of 5 other measures represented in Site Usage below, or compare two measures against each other.

- **Site Usage**: shows visits, total page views and pages per visit. The bounce rate indicates the percentage of visitors who left the site after viewing only one page. The average time on site excludes bounces since there's no way to measure the time spent if a user left immediately. New visits shows the percentage of visitors who had not visited the site previously. You can click any other of these six measures to drill down into more detail.

- **Map Overlay**: illustrates the geographic source of the visits. Click 'view report' to drill down further, showing state and city-level visitor information.

- **Traffic sources**: breaks down the visits into Direct (the URL was entered directly), Organic (it was followed from a search engine result), and major referral sites that have links to your site. The full report shows referral sites in more detail.

- **Content overview**: shows the most popular pages at a glance, based upon the number of pageviews.

- **Export/email**: here you can export reports or send emails either on a once-off basis or scheduled at regular intervals.

Visitors menu

Click Visitors on the left to open the submenu of options. There is a considerable amount of data here with some of the main highlights including:

- **Technical information**: the usage of different browsers, the connection speed of your users, their operating system, screen resolutions and support for features such as Java and Flash.

- **Benchmarking**: illustrates how your site compares to sites of a similar size.

- **Trending and loyalty**: over time this builds a picture of whether measures are improving or not, while loyalty shows the number of visitors who have visited n times, their length of visit and the depth of their search (how many pages were viewed).

Content menu

These reports are a gold mine for SEO opportunities, directly linking search terms with landing pages and user behavior. Some important parts include:

- **Top content**: the pages receiving the most number of pageviews.

- **Navigation summary**: how visitors moved around your site, where they came from and what they did next. There is also an entrance path analysis which shows the same for each page.

- **Top landing pages**: while most visitors likely arrive at the home page, high-ranking pages within your site will attract their own visits from organic search results (these are called landing pages).

- **Top exit pages**: discover which pages are making visitors leave the site. Ideally, an order confirmation page should have a high exit rate, while a shopping cart summary would be low.

- **Entrance keywords**: the most popular keywords and phrases that drew visitors to your site or specific webpage. The most successful phrases may not have been one you were intentionally targeting.

- **Site Overlay**: shows your site's home page and overlays click percentages, indicating which hyperlinks visitors followed.

Unlike any other analytics package, Google Analytics also provides deep integration with Google AdSense: incorporating cost-per-click pricing into this data providing an extra layer of information in calculating the return on investment for paid search.

Once you get started with Google Analytics, the features are practically limitless - A/B testing (showing different content to different visitors and comparing results), goal setting and intelligence reports and just some of powerful tools that give you an comprehensive insight into your web performance.

For comprehensive coverage of Google Analytics, read Google Analytics, 3rd Edition (ISBN 978-0470531280).

43 Know the myths of social media

Social media is a powerful marketing tool but it's no replacement for proven SEO strategies.

The way that your company and web site is viewed by the rest of the online world has a major impact of whether your site ranks well in search engine results. The explosive growth of social media networks has had such an effect on SEO that many now talk of Social Media Optimization (SMO) as the next step in its evolution as the two areas fuse together. While Twitter, Facebook and LinkedIn represent some of the most popular and well-known networks, there are many others that may be more useful in helping to promote your site, depending upon your industry.

Despite the fact that social media is discussed continuously in SEO circles, it isn't necessarily a panacea to all the obstacles we face in trying to rank on page one of the SERPs. While there are many examples of businesses that have undoubtedly flourished through the innovative use of Twitter or Facebook, there are also certain businesses that simply don't lend themselves to SMO. I believe that most sites shouldn't jettison their SEO efforts in favor of social media, so in this tip we will review the pitfalls and myths of social media in its relation to SEO and try to separate the fact from the fiction.

Social media isn't easy - or free.

Many businesses choose to focus on SEO instead of pay-per-click advertising since, at the most simplistic level, organic results in Google are 'free' and AdWords and similar PPC programs cost money. Similarly, social media is often seen as a replacement for SEO, offering a guarantee of almost endless traffic without the hard work needed in SEO to retain a number one ranking, but this view ignores all the problems:

- **Friendships are demanding**: as your social network grows, the amount of time needed to engage users and respond to questions increases substantially. While most of us can ignore chatter on our personal Facebook news feeds, if you're representing a brand or a business, you have to be constantly available to provide advice, handle complaints or criticisms and create new content to keep followers interested.

- **Everybody is a social media expert**, since there's no barrier to entry to opening a Twitter or Facebook account, and getting professional advice or social media management can be difficult. If social media is a major part of your online strategy, you will need professional consulting and full time help to continuously keep your audience engaged.

- **Results are extremely unpredictable**: unlike online advertising and SEO, where there is at least some correlation between effort and results, there are absolutely no guarantees in social media. Facebook applications are expensive to develop, viral videos can take time to produce with no guarantee of 'going viral', and generating content for Twitter can be exhausting - yet it's almost impossible to predict which campaigns will convert visitors into customers.

- **Success may be short-term**: typically, companies and customers are excited when they first connect over social media. But these interactions can rapidly fade, and even significant short-term success can evaporate if you even briefly take your finger off the mouse trigger, since people quickly forget about your brand. Long-term success takes consistent effort and persistent hard work, and it typically eludes most traditional attempts to measure ROI.

Avoiding the pitfalls of social media

Social media literacy has risen rapidly for individuals but awareness among organizations is still surprisingly low, and knowing the pitfalls is the first step to avoiding them:

- **Social media doesn't work for everyone**: typically, it's most successful in B2C, entertainment-driven or information-rich industries. Restaurants, bars, hotels, conferences and news organizations stand the greatest chance of success partly because their customers perceive what the industries provide as fun. Conversely, construction companies, law firms, insurers and potentially most B2B enterprises may struggle in finding and maintaining an audience.

- **Social marketing doesn't have a good ROI**: aside from high profile successes, most web sites would get a better return on their investment (considering both time and money) by focusing on SEO, pay-per-click advertising and conversion optimization. Social media can steadily supplement these but established practices with a measurable ROI shouldn't be neglected.

- **Social marketing is public relations**: the individuals you assign to manage your social marketing need to be highly experienced in representing your brand and public reputation. Organizations frequently hand off social media to the most junior employees, which can lead to inept messaging at best and public relations disasters in the worst cases.

A good social media strategy is much more than having a Facebook account and a Twitter logo added to your website. It involves constantly creating new engaging content from all levels of your organization, and integrating the efforts with SEO, online advertising and the traditional marketing plan.

For more information, read "The Social Media Bible: Tactics, Tools, and Strategies for Business Success" by Lon Safko and David Brake.

44 Add video as a content channel

Shooting video is no longer expensive and difficult, and yields ever-growing SEO benefits.

The days of text-only content are over: video is rapidly becoming the de facto type of content on web, and seems to be accelerating with the growth of Internet-enabled mobile devices. Whatever type of website you are running, you need to find a way to incorporate original video into your offering. While many business and website owners are deterred by the apparent complexity of "making a movie", or concerned with privacy issues - or simply embarrassment - they're missing out on a golden opportunity to build traffic.

Why does your site need video? YouTube search now represents 28% of all Google searches – visitors are actively seeking out videos as well as text. For "how to"-style articles, video is often more understandable than text, faster to create, and provide a higher rate of conversions.

Putting your face – or your CEO's and co-workers' faces – on a site also creates a rapport than helps differentiate your organization from competitors. In the social web, your visitors will be more involved if they can see who you are.

You may think you have nothing original to say on film, but some of the most popular video clips are about relatively mundane topics, such as the guide to upgrading Acer laptop memory which has received over 400,000 views (**http://www.youtube.com/watch?v=-EfzckyZMTk**). There are TV shows with lower ratings than this, but this video is compelling because it's an accurate and succinct guide to a complex problem which Acer laptop users couldn't solve.

Specific, relevant and informative videos receive the sort of traffic that many websites could never achieve. Regardless of your industry or profession, create a video that addresses the questions and needs of an audience. For example:

- **Chefs**: everyone would love to know how to chop vegetables quickly - show us how on video.

- **Realtors**: everybody wants the inside scoop on what to look forward in finding the perfect house - provide your best tips on film and place the video on your site.

- **Jewelers**: showcase your products and provide "How To" seminars on buying the best diamonds, or the appropriate stones for different wedding anniversaries.

What are the best practices for shooting video?

- **Transcribe the content**: search engines cannot index video content (yet) – providing a text transcript helps SEO and also allows viewers to skim for interesting sections of text to jump around the clip. One service that can do this for you is SpeakerText (**http://speakertext.com**).

- **Keep it short**: the optimal length for video is around 90 seconds, in terms of maximizing the number of viewers who will stay until the end. Clearly the length will depend on the subject matter, but the video should be no longer than it needs to be.

- **Invest in the audio**: audiences will watch sub-standard video with good audio, but not the other way around. Make sure the audio track is as clean as possible by using a external or lapel microphone that plugs into the camera.

- **Create a useful title**: just as the title *Titanic* communicates the topic to the audience effectively, your title will determine whether visitors view your video or not. And also whether it gets found by Google, so flex those keywords.

- **Create a video sitemap** for the best chance of your videos to be found by the crawlers and list it in your Google Webmaster Central account (see tip 41).

- **Host the video** on YouTube and embed the link on your site - YouTube will load-manage the media, and you will receive additional traffic to your site from referrals.

Rather than shooting commercials, which are more complicated and costly - and increasingly ignored by the audience - there are other types of video that are more useful to visitors and easier to create:

- **Interviews and testimonials**: with colleagues and co-workers, providing insights, expertise or breaking news around your business. For testimonials, ask customers to say how great your product or service is – it's more authentic on film that as a written statement on your site.

- **Testimonials**: **Screencasts**: for demonstrating either proprietary or third-party software, or how to work around problems with popular software. Visit **http://www.screentoaster.com** for a free online screen recorder.

- **How-to videos**: show your expertise by solving niche problems or providing advice in your field.

With an inexpensive HD camcorder, external microphone and basic video editing software, anyone can produce video content easily. Given the proliferation of cameras on devices, it's no surprise that video is becoming more important in the social context of web marketing. The direction that Google is taking with SEO also means that you ignore these trends at the risk of losing your existing ranking.

For tips on creating professional-looking footage, visit http://lifehacker. com/214043/8-ways-to-shoot-video-like-a-pro

45 **Start an Affiliate Program**

Boosting site traffic is at the core of SEO and affiliate marketing can help provide another channel.

For e-commerce websites, the cost of finding traffic and converting visitors into sales is known as the *cost of acquisition*. For SEO and SEM managers, one of the major goals is to keep this cost as low as possible, compared to the profitability margin of the product being sold. Affiliate programs offer a way of managing this cost by splitting the gross profit of sales with a range of third-party publishers who will advertise and promote the product on your behalf.

Affiliate programs are not suitable for every web site or industry, but for those that are high-margin, sales-driven and able to serve customers regardless of geography, they can open new sales channels. Additionally, a well-designed affiliate program that motivates, encourages and rewards affiliates can provide a major SEO benefit, since those third-parties will put significant effort into linking to your site and promoting online awareness.

There are several benefits to starting your own affiliate program:

- **Advertising costs are a percentage of sales**: unlike the variable costs of SEO, paid search or other per-per-click campaigns, affiliates receive a percentage of complete and settled sales (typically they receive no commission for returns). As your affiliate advertising cost increases, your sales are also increasing proportionally.

- **You minimize exposure to poorly-performing ads**: while affiliates have considerable latitude in promoting your products, they are experimenting to find the best-performing ads using their own budget. Even if you provide banners and ad copy to your affiliates, your own cost of acquisition remains constant regardless of how well those ads perform.

- **You can rapidly extend your reach**: while SEO and SEM campaigns take time to develop successfully, an affiliate program can attract hundreds of webmasters or publishers very quickly, exposing your product to much larger number of internet users.

Affiliate programs are successfully operated by large web retailers such as Amazon.com, Overstock, Hotels.com and there are thousands of smaller firms making substantial sales using this method. While there are many factors in developing a successful affiliate program, two of most important are to ensure the affiliate commission rate is sufficiently high to incentivize publishers, and to treat the top performers as an integral part of your sales team.

Affiliate networks

A successful affiliate program balances the needs and risks for both merchants and publishers. As a merchant, your major concerns are:

- **Finding quality publishers** who professionally market your products using legitimate marketing techniques, since customers often believe those sites directly represent your company. Publishers should make efforts to produce their own content, find their own niche markets and take steps not to compete directly with other affiliates or cannibalize your site's own sales through overly aggressive tactics.

- **Tracking and reporting**: just as with SEO and SEM, it's important to reliably track metrics such as number of impressions and click-through rates, so you can discover the most successful ad-copy, promotions and channels for your products.

Similarly, for affiliates making the effort to promote your products on a commission-only basis, these publishers also have requirements:

- **Accurate billing** is essential, so publishers can trust they are receiving commissions for the products they sell, and sales are reported honestly.

- **Timely communication**, with offers, promotions, new products and advertising materials provided by the merchant.

- **Incentives**, so the most successful affiliates receive a greater commission and bonuses for achieving specific targets.

Affiliate networks have developed as intermediaries between merchants and publishers in order to address these issues. Network membership is usually free for publishers, while merchants pay a set-up fee and ongoing commissions, but they enable merchants to reach a large range of publishers, and manage the complex issues of sending commissions to large numbers of affiliates.

Some of the biggest affiliate networks include Commission Junction (**http://www.cj.com**), Clickbank (**http://www.clickbank.com**) and Google Affiliate Network (**http://www.google.com/ads/affili-atenetwork**), though there are many others. These all offer a sizeable base of publishers, account support, advanced reporting tools and payment processing features, and should be a starting point if you are considering developing your own affiliate program.

For more information, read "A Practical Guide to Affiliate Marketing: Quick Reference for Affiliate Managers & Merchants" by Evgenii Prussakov.

46 **Using add-ons to automate SEO**

Take advantage of the growing number of free tools to help automate data collection in SEO.

Collecting data to help make SEO decisions is a major task, and one that involves significant time and manual effort, but fortunately there are tools available to help streamline some of these tasks. I've included this tip towards the end of the book because I think it's important to know how to collect the information manually as shown in earlier tips and understand what they mean before using add-ons and toolbars to speed up the process. While many of these work in other browsers, I would recommend installing Mozilla's FireFox browser at **http://www.mozilla.com**.

Alexa Toolbar

Alexa collects traffic information for the world's most popular websites together with search analytics, and you can either search for this information directly on their website or use the toolbar. Alexa's data is considered to be fairly reliable for larger websites, but not so useful for those with less traffic.

The toolbar appears above the page and automatically updates for every site you visit (see below). To install, go to **http://download.alexa.com** and click 'Install Alexa Toolbar'. Apart from showing the global ranking for websites based on site traffic, it also provides related links and the history of what a site looked like in the past using data from the WayBack Machine (**http://web.archive.org**).

The Alexa toolbar updates automatically for every site you visit.

SEO Quake

SEO Quake is another Firefox add-on available at **http://www.seoquake.com**, which loads a range of SEO metrics dynamically when a site is visited, disppearing in either the toolbar or an overlay as shown below.

You can configure the parameters shown within the application, but some of the most common are available in the default set provided, including:

- **PageRank**: the PR of the current page.

- **Index**: the number of pages in the site indexed in Google, Yahoo! and Bing.

- **Links**: how many inbound links are pointing to either the sub-domain or entire site, and the total number of internal and outbound links.

- **Statistics**: the age of the domain, Alexa rank, WhoIs domain data, keyword density, and estimated value of the domain name from SEMrush.

The plug-in can be configured to display a much broader range of SEO statistics and parameters but should be used with caution, since Google may temporarily block your IP address if you appear to be harvesting data for large numbers of sites. The one-page report available through the 'Info' button provides an SEO snapshot of a range of metrics, which is especially useful for analyzing both your own sites and those of competitors.

149

47 **Take advantage of email marketing**

Email is a highly effective way to draw traffic to your site but there are some important rules to follow.

According to the Direct Marketing Association, every $1 spent on email marketing in 2009 brought a $43 return, a statistic which compares very favorably with most other outbound marketing mechanisms. From an SEO perspective, email provides a important mechanism not only to introduce new potential customers to your site, but also to remind previous visitors to come back when you have new events, promotions or information.

Using one of the major email services on web, it's easy to create email campaigns as an inexpensive way to reach hundreds or thousands of recipients who have opted to hear from your organization. There are several steps involve from developing and maintaining a list of recipients, building effective emails that meet the needs of that list, and measuring the effectiveness of each campaign.

Developing a quality list of email addresses

The first challenge is to build up a list of email addresses, since the size and quality of the list will impact the effectiveness of each campaign. There are several ways to do this:

- **Add sign-up forms on your website**: most email services offer widgets that make it easy to embed a sign-up form anywhere on your site. Even with a small percentage of visitors choosing to sign-up, it's possible to build a large list of subscribers relatively quickly.

- **Providing email opt-ins at your place of business**: from low-tech "free lunch draws" to asking customers to subscribe at the point-of-sale, it's simple to provide incentives that allow existing customers to join your list.

- **Provide a link to an email sign-form** in the signature of outgoing emails, and add "Forward to a friend" to links to marketing messages. Anywhere you currently communicate with potential clients, provide an invitation to join.

It's important to remember the importance of asking permission when building an email list. Although direct marketers in the offline world frequently flaunt the "Do Not Call" list and will send junk mail indiscriminately, the CAN-SPAM Act in the United States (and similar acts in other countries) makes it illegal to send email solicitations without consent. Even if it's not illegal, it's bad for your brand reputation to harvest email addresses using any method where the sender is not explicitly choosing to receive your marketing messages. Whether you collect email addresses online or offline::

- **Use a double opt-in procedure**, which send a confirmation email requesting that the recipient agrees to future email messaging from your company.

- **Provide a single-click unsubscribe link** so recipients can remove themselves at any time.

- **Provide your business name and address** on each communication, which may be legally required in your jurisdiction, but also makes the message more credible.

Using an email marketing service

Since sending email is free, many marketers wonder why they should pay for a service to send the emails on their behalf. There are several important reasons that make these services essential for any serious marketer:

- **List management**: they handle the exhaustive task of managing subscriptions and removals. There's a high churn rate in email marketing so this feature alone is major time-saver.

- **Compliance** with the laws mentioned above: any major service now keeps your messages in compliance with the basic requirements.

- **Ensuring privacy**: I've seen companies 'cc' hundreds of email addresses, giving everyone access to the entire campaign list. This shows an extraordinary disregard for the privacy that users have come to expect and leads to unsubscribes and complaints. While this is usually a mistake (the sender intended to 'bcc' rather than 'cc'), using an email service will guarantee this never happens because they dispatch emails one at a time.

- **Templates**: building good-looking HTML is not easy, and email services usually host a wide selection of professional templates that are easy to customize.

- **Reporting**: tracking how many recipients open emails and follow the clicks is not easy to do manually, but email services provide these features as standard.

There are a wide variety of email services available and some of the most popular include:

- **Constant Contact** (http://www.constantcontact.com)

- **Vertical Response** (http://www.verticalresponse.com)

- **Mail Chimp** (http://www.mailchimp.com)

- **AWeber** (http://www.aweber.com), which is particularly good for multi-part and staged email communications to follow-up with recipients at preset intervals.

Building effective email campaigns

Possibly the most important factor is the frequency of campaigns. Everybody receives too much email, so it's critical to send messages only when you have something that's important and useful to say. While there's no rule to decide how often is too often, deluging customers' mailboxes with bland, repetitious or untargeted messages is one sure way to alienate users. The goal is to get as many people to visit your site and act upon your message as possible - not to deter them through spam.

Crafting an email is an art and a science and there are some rules you should follow to maximize your open and click-through rates:

- **Subject line**: most email clients pile email into one long list of subject lines, so help people decide what to read by making the subject line direct, honest and short. The average person has learned to detest and avoid sensationalist headlines (e.g. "JAMES, YOU MUST READ THIS!!!").

- **Sender name**: it's more effective to send the email from a person in your organization that a generic and faceless account such as *info* or *donotreply*. You should also check the sender account for responses - it surprises me how many marketers invade inboxes from unmonitored accounts and believe that creates support for their brand.

- **Images and HTML**: images work well in email, but some recipients have these disabled (or use cell phones where text is easier to read), so provide emails in both HTML and text format.

- **Get to the point**: state your message in the first paragraph and provide a call to action. You have between 5 and 30 seconds to get a response so if you want the recipient to call, click or take some other action, ask them to do so as fast as possible.

- **Personalization**: while including the recipient's first name isn't that important anymore, I do think the message should be tailored appropriately. With a large email list it's easy to blast out anonymous messages but they come across as untargeted and irrelevant. Take the time to segment your list and provide messages that are useful to various groups.

- **Check your rendering**: unfortunately, the way email clients show messages is less standardized than how browsers show web pages, and an email that looks good in Gmail may be broken in Microsoft Outlook. There are many popular email clients, so the easiest way to test is to use a service like Email On Acid (**http://www.emailonacid.com**) which will render your email in 15 different clients and help find problems before the campaign is sent.

- **Avoid attachments**: including PDFs or other files is a mistake - these fill mailboxes, make emails slow to send and make it impossible to see who opened the attachment, or even to replace the attachment if there's an error. Instead, include a link to the attachment hosted on your server.

As everyone with an email account has discovered, spam is a major problem so there is automated software used by email providers to judge whether messages are legitimate or not. When this software flags your messages as spam (or users report your messages), the credibility of your current and futures campaigns suffers, and ultimately your domain can end up blacklisted.

You must avoid words and phrases that sound like spam such as free, affordable, check, urgent, etc. For a review of words and phrases that typically trigger the spam filters, see **http://blog.mannixmarketing.com/2009/08/spam-trigger-words**. And before sending, always check your email with your email services' spam detector.

Fine-tuning your email campaigns

The goal of any email campaign is to encourage recipients to open a message and click links that lead back to landing pages back on your website. Once the user reaches the website, ideally they will navigate further, make purchases, bookmark your site and remember to come back in the future. All of these positive results increase the popularity of the site and increase the chance of users sharing content and links.

Building a successful email marketing strategy takes time, and can be fine-tuned based upon the feedback that develops over multiple campaigns. To help build a picture of which campaigns are having the most impact, use the reporting tools in your email service to monitor several important metrics:

- **Open rates**, which are typically quite low, but can be affected by the quality of the subject line and the time or day that the email was sent. If your email list has grown substantially and this measure has fallen, you should review the list quality to ensure the recipients have opted in.

- **Click-through rates** are provided for each hyperlink contained in the email. Usually, the links at the top of the email receive the highest CTR and hyperlinked images are the lowest. Ensure that links are obvious to readers, and break up longer stories with 'Read more' links to bring the reader back to your website.

- **Bounces** indicate email addresses that are no longer working and should be removed from your database of recipients as part of regular cleansing and list maintenance.

- **Unsubscribes** show how many users no longer want to hear from you, and if this number starts to grow can indicate that your messages are not useful or relevant to your audience.

For more information on email marketing, read "Successful Email Marketing Strategies" by Arthur Hughes and Arthur Sweetser.

48 **Ask for help when you need it**

It's important to have hands-on SEO knowledge, but there are times when hiring an expert can pay off.

I think it's essential for any modern marketing department or entrepreneur to have an in-depth and up to date knowledge of the best practices to build their online presence. Unlike many other services a business would use, such as legal or accounting, most companies should use SEO consultants to grow their own knowledge and steer their own online marketing plans. In other words, using an SEO professional should not be an excuse to hand off all the work - it should be a partnership to help improve your business' skills internally, and provide assistance where needed.

At the same time, keeping everything in-house won't lead to the best results in the long term - SEO strategies are fast changing, and there's considerable time and effort in maintaining and building a web presence. There are times when you will want and need to get outside help in bringing your SEO efforts back on track, marketing for a particular campaign, or just dealing with resource constraints.

There are many SEO companies out there, some of which are world-class and others of which are not so good. When you hire experts to help out with your SEO, do your homework to make sure your existing effort will not be squandered - it's easier to go backwards in search engine rankings than forwards, and undoing mistakes can take considerable time. As when hiring anyone, the first step is to ask plenty of questions:

- What strategies do you employ to improve rankings? Should I expect a project customized to my web site and industry or a generic approach that could be applied anywhere?

- What do you expect the ROI to be? What has been your typical ROI on previous projects? How to your intend to measure and report the efforts of your SEO work?

- What support do you need from our side to complete this project? How do you intend to communicate with our team?

- What previous work can you show me? Can you demonstrate that your SEO strategy made a measurable impact?

- What are the risks involved with your proposals? What's the potential downside, how can you mitigate risks and what will you do if our rankings deteriorate?

- How will you bill hours and what are your invoice terms?

- Are you outsourcing work to any third party and if so why?

Additionally, look at details that help establish their credibility and trustworthiness such as:

- Professional references/referrals.
- Education and work history.
- Gut instinct and impressions from meetings.
- Opinions of others knowledgeable in related fields.
- Description of billing, charging and planned work.

Companies that mention guaranteed rankings, unrealistic levels of traffic, auto-submissions or link exchanges should be avoided, and any SEO expert worth his or her salt will pledge (in writing) to never use "blackhat" methods such as those discussed in this book.

Pricing is a good indicator here, since $99 guarantees to rank #1 on Google can only be achieved by less-than-ideal methods. One common trick is to rank for long-tail phrases that nobody searches on - it's easy to list number one for "Jane Doe's Amazing Beauty Products" but the amount of traffic will be non-existent. Once again, understanding the proposed methods and the scope of the project should uncover these kinds of shenanigans. More nefarious SEO practices can irreparably damage your site and reputation, so interview plenty of candidate companies and check backgrounds before moving forward.

Red flags

As a competitive business, it's true that there's a good amount of over-promising and under-delivering in the SEO world. But clients can be difficult too, and many SEO professionals also look for red flags in potential customer contracts, some of which include:

- **Unrealistic expectations** and a belief in back-door SEO tricks that yield instant results. SEO takes time and it's good to avoid clients who don't recognize this.
- **Indecisiveness**: are you hiring an SEO company or not? Many companies sit on the fence and endlessly debate the pros and cons. Unfortunately these same clients often have a crippling inability to make recommended changes to their sites, thus sabotaging the SEO effort.
- **Politics**: SEO is a little design, a little technology and a lot of measuring and tweaking. It has the ability to aggravate designers, marketers and IT, and some companies are not cut out for this.

Every company large or small should have a clear online marketing strategy, part of which should be SEO. Once this is formulated and parts of the organization are aligned to maximum their online presence to generate traffic and customers, these issues tend not to be a problem.

49 Keep up with SEO industry news

Like any highly competitive business, the way to stay ahead is to keep up with the industry's cutting edge.

A little history

SEO is a young industry that only started to emerge in the mid 1990s. In the early days of Yahoo!, if you had a reasonably average site, you could reliably get first page placement just by submitting your URL. The algorithmic side of search engine design didn't emerge until around 1996, which gave birth to keyword density, data mining and other concepts to detect topical relevance within web pages. It wasn't long after that crackers had decoded the ranking factors of the early crawlers, and could game the system to dominate keyword phrases at will.

By the end of 1997, spammers had essentially rendered the early search engines useless, and Hotbot and Infoseek - two of the big names back then - were riddled with irrelevant results. Up until 2000, the arms race between search engines and spammers intensified, culminating in more and more ranking metrics becoming "off-site factors", largely beyond the control of those who were tricking the system.

And then Google arrived with their PageRank concept, determining that sites that were hubs or authorities should have precedence above those they were standalone or without a reputation. This seimic shift changed the way search engines worked forever, causing an exodus of users from Excite, Altavista, HotBot, Yahoo! and AOL. Google quickly solidified their number one position by consistently provided timely and relevant results, and in the coming years refined their algorithms to weed out the malicious sites and reward those that were content-rich and user-centric.

Many of the previous tricks - keyword stuffing, doorway pages, duplicate content, cloaking and link exchanges - rapidly became signals for search engines to ban sites and delist them forever. Meanwhile, legitimate sites became more aware of user behavior, pay-per-click advertising and growing an online reputation. All the while, SEO has been divided into two camps: statisticians and programmers who attempt to reverse engineer the inner workings of Googlebot, and those that continue to peddle misinformation on unsuspecting clients.

After 15 years of practically non-stop industry reinvention, the web is maturing and both search engines and optimizers must keep looking forward to stay number one. At the end of the day, both thrive and survive on meeting the needs of their users.

Looking ahead

Even in the last couple of years, there have been enormous changes in search engine technology, moving towards the real time information and the *semantic web*. As website designers, business owners and search engine optimizers, all of us have to stay constantly alert for these changes and how they impact:

- **Visitors**: how are visitors going to find your site? Will users continue to use search engines or expect social networks to find relevance more easily?

- **Channels**: as everything electronic becomes connected to the web, will desktop, mobile, TV or some other device become the most important in reaching potential customers?

- **Search engines**: will the social graph developed by friendship trees replace the link graph that's currently one of the founding pillars of SEO?

With so many things changing, you have to keep abreast of changes to ensure your website retains its high rankings. Since search engines don't provide much information about how their proprietary algorithms work, one of the best ways to do this is to watch the industry experts who try to decode the changes and provide advice on best practices. There are hundreds of SEO blogs and websites, but for your continuing SEO education, here are some of the ones you should watch closely:

- Search Engine Land (**http://www.searchengineland.com**)
- SEOmoz (**http://www.SEOmoz.org**)
- Pepperjam's Blog (**http://www.pepperjam.com/blog**)
- Graywolf's SEO Blog (**http://www.wolf-howl.com**)
- Stuntdubl.com (**http://stuntdubl.com**)
- Jim Boykin (**http://www.jimboykin.com**)
- David Naylor (**http://www.davidnaylor.co.uk**)
- Search Engine Journal (**http://www.searchenginejournal.com**)
- Search Engine Guide (**http://www.searchengineguide.com**)
- Webmaster World (**http://www.webmasterworld.com**)
- WebProNews (**http://www.webpronews.com**)

Social networks are also a good source for SEO ideas - don't forget to check LinkedIn's groups at http://linkedin.com/groups.

50 Know the SEO Myths

There's plenty of misinformation about how SEO works: here are some of the most common erroneous claims.

Don't put all your sites on the same server or IP address or Google will take you down.

For the average person running a few sites, this isn't a problem. Search engines target servers hosting hundreds and thousands of sites for the sake of artificially creating content. For most people, this isn't something they should worry about. Of course, the tolerance question of how many sites is "too many" is not public information, but it's likely to be a large number.

Google penalizes you for including Javascript files that are hosted on a different site.

Hosting Javascript on a separate site is a very common practice - even Google Analytics and Google AdSense use this technique. Some spam sites are caught for the way they use Javascript to perform redirects, but this isn't something that would affect any legitimate site. If you include scripts from other sites, while it's possible this will have a negative effect on your load time, it won't effect search engine rankings.

Using the robots.txt file is the only way to stop a page or site being crawled by a search spider.

Robots.txt is 'politely observed' by search engine spiders, but there's no guarantee it will be honored. Spambots and other spiders may disregard the file completely, or use it as a guide to files and folders you are trying to protect. The best protection is to use the .htaccess file or features within your CMS to add password protection to the pages or directories you want to block.

You can make Google crawl your site more often by changing the setting in Google Webmaster Tools.

Although there is a manual setting in GWT (see tip 41), Google decides its own crawl rate so the manual setting cannot be used to make it happen more often. The only way to achieve this is to produce new relevant content more frequently.

Outbound links to quality and authoritative sites improve your Google PageRank.

Sadly not - while it's good practice to link to useful resources within your pages, and certain visitors will thank you for the references, it doesn't help either your ranking in search results or PageRank. If it did, everyone would jam their pages with thousands of relevant links. On the flip side, having too many outbound links can cause your pages to be identified as spam.

You can't rank number one for a keyword phrase without a high PageRank.

Search engine results placement and PageRank are not connected. It's possible to have a PR1 page rank first for a given phrase, or a PR9 page not rank at all. PageRank is an indication of likely quality and authority and nothing else (and although it's calculated constantly, these updates are not published publicly very often, so you won't see it change as your pages are updated).

You must submit your URL to Google and other search engines to get listed.

The best way to appear in Google is to get another indexed page to link to yours. The Google Add tool (**http://www.google.com/addurl**) doesn't make any guarantees that the site will be added to the index, and - anecdotally - doesn't seem to do very much at all. In all three major search engines, I've found that inbound links from sites that have a history in the indexes are the best way for quick indexing.

SEO can be done in a month.

Unfortunately, SEO takes time because the search engines don't respond instantaneously, and they want to see a history of relevant content and deep links from quality sites to yours. It takes time to build this online reputation, and then continuous effort to maintain a top ranking. SEO takes time to plan and implement, and even longer to maintain. One month is an arbitrary time frame, and a more realistic period of time would depend on your site's goals.

Your click-through rate determines your ranking.

The click-through rate is the number of times visitors click through to a website in search results. The major engines have publicly said they don't use this metric, claiming it's statistically noisy and not particularly useful.

You can only get top ranking if you use an engine's paid search.

This rumor won't die, but for the record having a Google AdWords campaign won't improve the organic search results of your SEO. Think about it - the biggest companies have the biggest budgets for paid search, yet they don't dominate most search results. More importantly, if there was a connection between paid and organic search as this rumor implies, search engines would lose business for placing dollar revenue (which visitors don't care about) above relevance (which visitors do care about).

You might well benefit from paid search in all sorts of ways, but improvement in organic rankings won't be one of them.

SEO is dead.

No, SEO is changing - dramatically - but it's definitely far from dead. Off page factors, social media and the changing way content is produced and consumed all have profound effects on optimization. Techniques that worked 5 years ago mostly don't work anymore but, as with so many things on the web, the state of flux means you have to stay current with best practices.

SEO is practiced effectively by more and more websites, which means the simple ways to get to the top have already been done for many industries. This means you have to use all the tips and techniques at your disposal to give your site the best chances of ranking on the first page for your chosen keywords. This book summarizes what I currently consider the best methods - but than could all change in a year's time!

Only inbound links with high PageRank (PR) will help bring traffic to your site.

When a page with a high PR links to a page on your site, your page will receive an increase in its PageRank score. For example, a page with a PR of 6 linking to a page previously with a PR of 2 may well increase the PR to 3 or 4. But PageRank is an indication of authority and does not bring traffic or necessarily increase your page's position in the search results. By itself, an inbound link from a high PR page has very little to do with traffic. Instead you should focus on relevant sites in your niche that receive high traffic - getting an inbound links from these pages will bring additional visitors.

The best way to boost traffic is to get thousands of inbound links.

Having hundreds or thousands of inbound links from low quality websites will do nothing to help your reputation with search engines, and may even make you look like a spammer. You do need backlinks, but only ones from quality, relevant sites will make a difference to your SEO. It's better to have

50 average quality inbound links or a dozen high quality ones to make a big difference. It's easy to buy software that will find thousands of links for your site but, as usual in SEO, the quick and lazy way will not yield any long-term benefits.

You must repeat keywords in the keywords meta tag, and repeat them for <insert your percentage here>% through the copy.

The meta keywords tag isn't used in any meaningful way by search engines (except to identify likely spammers who fill the tags with repetitious phrases). While some crawlers may use it, Google, Yahoo! and Bing are your target engines and it won't have any influence on them. If SEO was as simple as stuffing keywords into tags, search engine results would quickly become filled with spam.

As for the keyword density argument, this has been circulating for years and really doesn't work anymore. The idea is that keywords should represent a percentage of the total numbers of words on each page, and is usually quoted as 3-6%. Following this practice leads to web copy that annoys your visitors at best, and may get your site flagged for spam at worst. While you should use your keywords on your pages, don't obsess with keyword density - just write naturally and normally and search engines will understand.

Having dozens of domain names pointing to one site helps your SEO - if 1 site is good, 50 sites is better.

Almost everyone I know in web design owns dozens of sites, many pointing to one original site. Even though the domains may be keyword rich, this leads to duplicate content issues (see tip 28) unless each domain has its own unique content. Given the work in optimizing one site, I'd argue that it's really not worth the effort to attempt to optimize 10 sites all around the same topic.

If you have several domain points to the same place for marketing purposes (e.g. http://bestbuilders.com points to http://xyzconstruction.com), this is fine as long as you have 301 redirects in place. Also, if you have a multinational company with domains in different countries, there are ways to handle this too without problems (see **http://googlewebmastercentral.blogspot.com/2010/03/working-with-multi-regional-websites.html** for details).

Having multiple domains pointing to the same place doesn't improve SEO - for most sites it's better to buy a great domain name when you start out, and focus all your efforts on that site's content.

If you hear any good SEO rumors, email me at james@ranking-number1.com and I'll be happy to help. Thanks for reading!

8993798R0

Made in the USA
Lexington, KY
20 March 2011